THE UNSEEN REALM

A Question & Answer Companion

T0311477

THE UNSEEN REALM

A Question & Answer Companion

Douglas Van Dorn

LEXHAM PRESS

The Unseen Realm: A Question & Answer Companion

Copyright 2016 Douglas Van Dorn

Lexham Press, 1313 Commercial St., Bellingham, WA 98225
LexhamPress.com

Print ISBN 9781577996934
Digital ISBN 9781577996927

Lexham Editorial Team: Lynnea Fraser, Spencer Jones

Typesetting: ProjectLuz.com

CONTENTS

The target audience for Dr. Michael Heiser's recent book *The Unseen Realm: Recovering the Supernatural Worldview of the Bible* was primarily the academic reader—pastors and professionals in other fields accustomed to digesting closely researched material. While *The Unseen Realm* is nevertheless quite readable, this primer meets the need for a more accessible abridgement of *The Unseen Realm's* core content.

This question and answer companion introduces and summarizes major content elements of Dr. Heiser's book in 10 sections by means of a question–answer format. However, the primer does not follow the chapter sequence of *The Unseen Realm*, nor does it touch on everything discussed.

It's time to read the Bible for what it is: a grand, unified story that involves the intersection of the unseen realm with human history not only in the distant past, but also with us today. Recently the Bible has too often been presented to congregations as something much less: a self-help manual for successful living, a motivational trade book, a guide for relationships, a handy source of character sketches, etc. This primer seeks to correct these errant approaches.

To that end, the primer is arranged in the following sections:

- Part I begins with God. We must start here, to ground ourselves, for he is the Beginning and the End, the Creator, and the Savior. So we ask questions like who is he? What has he done? What is his nature? How does he reveal himself?

- Part II addresses the gods of the nations, rivals to Yahweh, and the God of Israel. Do these gods really exist? If so, what are they? How does God compare to gods? What distinguishes him from them? Why are none of them comparable to him?

- Part III focuses on one phrase: sons of God. Who are they? How do they relate to other heavenly beings? What is the Son of God's (that is, Jesus') relationship to other sons of God? How does this biblical phrase relate to other biblical terminology, such as angels, watchers, cherubim, and more?

- Part IV introduces a very important topic that is unfamiliar to most non-specialists: the divine council. The term comes from Psalm 82:1 and is therefore part of how the Bible depicts the bureaucratic operation of God's heavenly host and how that divine council impacts us on earth.

- Part V deals with the earth and its relationship to the divine realm. It discusses Adam and Eve's creation, their fall into sin, and the divine being that tempted Eve. This section also asks about the image of God (What is it? What function and purpose did God create Adam to carry out?), along with the results of the fall.

- Part VI develops the biblical story of the long conflict between the spiritual and earthly realms by examining the divine rebellion of Gen 6:1-4. This passage describes a transgression of the boundary between heaven and earth and its consequences in later biblical history, particularly the conquest of Canaan under Moses and Joshua. This section concentrates on the biblical giants, the Nephilim, along with their descendants, the giant clans of Canaan.

- Part VII focuses on the human rebellion against God after the flood—the Tower of Babel. This event frames the rest of biblical history in both Testaments. The section focuses on the cosmic-geographical worldview resulting from God's judgment—disinheriting the nations and allotting them to lesser gods.

- Part VIII proceeds to examine how this cosmic conflict relates to the promise given to Eve in the garden of Eden, that one of her offspring—the promised seed—would eventually undo the failure in Eden.

- Part IX explores the fulfillment of the promised seed in Jesus Christ—how his coming, his work at the cross, his resurrection, and his ascension to the right hand of God dealt a powerful blow to Satan, the lesser gods, and demons.

- Part X concludes the primer with an examination of the gospel, the good news of God's plan of salvation and the demise of the powers of darkness and their rule.

My hope is that this primer will lead all who read it and use it in ministry to a deeper understanding of the supernatural worldview of the Bible and a greater love for the Triune God who has won the war through his Son, Jesus Christ.

May the Lord of Lords and God of gods, with whom no power on heaven or earth can compare, be pleased to use this tool for the furtherance of his glory alone, and may he be pleased through it to help you worship him alone as the true God, especially as he has revealed himself to us through the Son and through the Holy Spirit, sent to lead us into all truth.

Soli Deo Gloria (to God alone be the glory),

—Douglas Van Dorn

Scripture citations are from the English Standard Version (ESV) unless otherwise noted. In many cases, only the most relevant portion of a verse is quoted, but the reader should feel free to look up the biblical passages to get the fullest context. The Scripture passages cited are not necessarily those used in *The Unseen Realm* to establish or discuss any specific point.

Select footnotes clarify a point or direct the readers to resources for further study.

NIV	New International Version
ESV	English Standard Version
JPS	Jewish Publication Society's English Tanakh
LXX	Septuagint
NASB	New American Standard Bible
NET	the NET Bible
DDD	*Dictionary of Deity and Demons in the Bible*
HALOT	*The Hebrew and Aramaic Lexicon of the Old Testament*

PART 1

GOD

Question 1. Who made us?

The LORD God made us.

> **Gen 2:7**. Then the LORD God formed the man of dust from the ground and breathed into his nostrils the breath of life, and the man became a living creature.

> **Pss 100:3-4**. Know that the LORD, he is God! It is he who made us, and we are his; we are his people, and the sheep of his pasture.

> **Pss 119:73**. Your hands have made and fashioned me; give me understanding that I may learn your commandments.

Question 2. What else did the LORD God make?

The LORD God made all things in heaven and on earth, both visible and invisible.

> **Isa 44:24**. Thus says the LORD, your Redeemer, who formed you from the womb: "I am the LORD, who made

all things, who alone stretched out the heavens, who spread out the earth by myself."

John 1:1-3. In the beginning was the Word, and the Word was with God, and the Word was God. He was in the beginning with God. All things were made through him, and without him was not anything made that was made.

Col 1:16. For by him all things were created, in heaven and on earth, visible and invisible, whether thrones or dominions or rulers or authorities—all things were created through him and for him.

Heb 1:2. In these last days [God] has spoken to us by his Son, whom he appointed the heir of all things, through whom also he created the world.

Question 3. What is God?

God is spirit.

Deut 4:12. Then the LORD spoke to you out of the midst of the fire. You heard the sound of words, but saw no form; there was only a voice.

Isa 31:3. The Egyptians are man, and not God, and their horses are flesh, and not spirit.

John 4:24. God is spirit, and those who worship him must worship in spirit and truth.

Acts 17:29. We ought not to think that the divine being is like gold or silver or stone, an image formed by the art and imagination of man.

Question 4. How does God exist?

God exists as one eternal uncreated being,[a] in three eternally distinct persons.[b]

[a] **Mark 12:29**. Jesus answered, "The most important [law] is, 'Hear, O Israel: The Lord our God, the Lord is one' " (quoting Deut 6:4).

Gal 3:20. An intermediary implies more than one, but God is one.

Jas 2:19. You believe that God is one; you do well. Even the demons believe—and shudder!

[b] **Matt 3:16–17**. And when Jesus was baptized, immediately he went up from the water, and behold, the heavens were opened to him, and he saw the Spirit of God descending like a dove and coming to rest on him; and behold, a voice from heaven said, "This is my beloved Son, with whom I am well pleased."

Matt 28:19. Go therefore and make disciples of all nations, baptizing them in the name of the Father and of the Son and of the Holy Spirit.

2 Cor 13:14. The grace of the Lord Jesus Christ and the love of God and the fellowship of the Holy Spirit be with you all.

1 Pet 1:2. According to the foreknowledge of God the Father, in the sanctification of the Spirit, for obedience to Jesus Christ and for sprinkling with his blood.

Question 5. Who are these three persons of the Godhead?

The three persons of the Godhead are God the Father,[a] God the Son,[b] and God the Holy Spirit.[c]

[a] **Deut 32:6**. Is he not your father, who created you, who made you and established you?"

Pss 89:26. You are my Father, my God, and the Rock of my salvation.

Isa 63:16. You are our Father … O LORD, our Father, our Redeemer from of old is your name.

Matt 6:9. Our Father in heaven, hallowed be your name.

Matt 16:17. Flesh and blood has not revealed this to you, but my Father who is in heaven.

Gal 1:1. Through Jesus Christ and God the Father, who raised him from the dead.

[b] **Pss 2:12**. Kiss the Son, lest he be angry, and you perish in the way.

John 1:1–3. In the beginning was the Word, and the Word was with God, and the Word was God.

John 1:17–18. For the law was given through Moses; grace and truth came through Jesus Christ. No one has ever seen God; the only God, who is at the Father's side, he has made him known.

Rom 9:5. The Christ who is God over all, blessed forever. Amen.

Heb 1:2. In these last days he has spoken to us by his Son, whom he appointed the heir of all things, through whom also he created the world.

c **Gen 1:2**. The Spirit of God was hovering over the face of the waters.

Acts 5:3-4. Why has Satan filled your heart to lie to the Holy Spirit ... You have not lied to men but to God.

1 Cor 2:11. So also no one comprehends the thoughts of God except the Spirit of God.

Question 6. Why is the first person called "Father"?

God the Father is the personal source of all things,[a] the king of his creation,[b] and from him proceed the Son and the Spirit.[c]

a **Acts 17:28**. In him we live and move and have our being.

Rom 11:36. For from him and through him and to him are all things. To him be glory forever. Amen.

b **1 Tim 1:17**. To the King of ages, immortal, invisible, the only God, be honor and glory forever and ever. Amen.

1 Tim 6:15-16. He who is the blessed and only Sovereign, the King of kings and Lord of lords, who alone has immortality, who dwells in unapproachable light, whom no one has ever seen or can see. To him be honor and eternal dominion. Amen.

ᶜ **John 1:14**. The Word became flesh, and dwelt among us, and we beheld his glory, glory as of the only begotten from the Father, full of grace and truth.

John 15:26. But when the Helper comes, whom I will send to you from the Father, the Spirit of truth, who proceeds from the Father, he will bear witness about me.

Question 7. Why is the second person called "Son"?

The Son proceeds from the Father[a] and is the great prince[b] and king[c] through whom the Father creates and upholds all things.[d]

ᵃ **John 1:14**. The Word became flesh, and dwelt among us, and we beheld his glory, glory as of the only begotten from the Father, full of grace and truth.

Heb 1:5. For to which of the angels did God ever say, "You are my Son, today I have begotten you"? Or again, "I will be to him a father, and he shall be to me a son"? (quoting Pss 2:7; 2 Sam 7:14).

ᵇ **Isa 9:6**. His name shall be called Wonderful Counselor, Mighty God, Everlasting Father, Prince of Peace.

Dan 12:1. At that time shall arise Michael, the great prince who has charge of your people [Israel].[1]

c **Pss 2:6-7**. As for me, I have set my King on Zion, my holy hill." I will tell of the decree: The LORD said to me, "You are my Son; today I have begotten you."

John 12:15. Fear not, daughter of Zion; behold, your king is coming, sitting on a donkey's colt! (quoting Zech 9:9).

Acts 5:31. God exalted him at his right hand as Leader and Savior, to give repentance to Israel and forgiveness of sins.

Rev 19:16. On his robe and on his thigh he has a name written, King of kings and Lord of lords.

d **John 1:1, 3**. In the beginning was the Word, and the Word was with God, and the Word was God. ... All things were made through him, and without him was not any thing made that was made.

---

1. This is a debateable point and therefore disputable prooftext. Some OT scholars still take up an ancient view that identifies Michael with the preincarnate Christ (see Meredith Kline, "The Servant and the Serpent," Kerux 8/1 (May 1993): 20–37, especially n. 11). While this is a view that Dr. Heiser does not adopt, I take this view, though not dogmatically. J. J. Collins summarizes why the view persists, "It should be noted that in the Hebrew Bible prior to Daniel, the Lord serves as ruler of Israel, a role given to Michael here" (John Joseph Collins and Adela Yarbro Collins, *Daniel: A Commentary on the Book of Daniel* (Hermeneia; Minneapolis, MN: Fortress Press, 1993), 375; see also 318).

Col 1:16. For by him all things were created, in heaven and on earth, visible and invisible, whether thrones or dominions or rulers or authorities—all things were created through him and for him.

1 Cor 8:6. Yet for us there is one God, the Father, from whom are all things and for whom we exist, and one Lord, Jesus Christ, through whom are all things and through whom we exist.

Question 8. Why is the third person called the "Holy Spirit"?

The Holy Spirit proceeds from the Father and the Son[a] and is the breath of God's Word,[b; 2] the giver of life.[c]

a **John 15:26.** But when the Helper comes, whom I will send to you from the Father, the Spirit of truth, who proceeds from the Father, he will bear witness about me.

b **Gen 2:7.** The LORD God formed the man of dust from the ground and breathed into his nostrils the breath of life, and the man became a living creature.

Job 4:9. By the breath of God they perish, and by the blast of his anger they are consumed.

---

2. The Hebrew word for "spirit" and "breath" are the identical word *ruah*.

Job 33:4. The Spirit of God has made me, and the breath of the Almighty gives me life.

c **Rom 8:10**. If Christ is in you, although the body is dead because of sin, the Spirit is life because of righteousness.

2 Cor 3:6. The Spirit gives life.

Question 9. How does God chiefly reveal himself?

God chiefly reveals himself through his Name[a] and his Word.[b]

a **Exod 33:19**. I will make all my goodness pass before you and will proclaim before you my name 'The LORD.'

Isa 7:14. The Lord himself will give you a sign. Behold, the virgin shall conceive and bear a son, and shall call his name Immanuel.

b **Gen 15:1**. After these things the word of the LORD came to Abram in a vision: "Fear not, Abram, I am your shield; your reward shall be very great."

1 Sam 15:10. The word of the LORD came to Samuel.

John 1:14. The Word became flesh.

Heb 1:1-2. Long ago, at many times and in many ways, God spoke to our fathers by the prophets, but in these last days he has spoken to us by his Son.

Question 10. What is the Name of God?

The Name of God is God; the Name appears in the Old Testament as the angel-word of the LORD;[a] in the New Testament the Name was incarnated in the womb of the virgin Mary and was named Jesus Christ,[b] fully human and fully God. In both he is the second person of the Holy Trinity.[3]

[a] **Gen 48:15-16.** And he blessed Joseph and said, "*The God* before whom my fathers Abraham and Isaac walked, *the God* who has been my shepherd all my life long to this day, *the angel* who has redeemed me from all evil, bless the boys.[4]

Exod 3:2, 4, 13-14. The angel of the LORD appeared to [Moses] in a flame of fire out of the midst of a bush ... When the LORD saw that [Moses] turned aside to see, God called to him out of the bush ... Then Moses said to God, "If I come to the people of Israel and say to them, 'The God of your fathers has sent me to you,' and they ask me, 'What is his name?' what shall I say to them?" God said to Moses, "I AM WHO I AM." And he said, "Say this to the people of Israel, 'I AM has sent me to you.' "

Exod 23:20-21. Behold, I send an angel before you to guard you on the way and to bring you to the place that

---

3. See *The Unseen Realm*, Chapters 16–18.
4. Empahsis added. The verb "bless" is grammatically singular in Hebrew, thereby identifying the Angel with God.

I have prepared. Pay careful attention to him and obey his voice; do not rebel against him, for he will not pardon your transgression, for my name is in him.

Deut 4:37. [God] brought you out of Egypt with his own presence, by his great power.

Judg 2:1. Now the angel of the LORD went up from Gilgal to Bochim. And he said, "I brought you up from Egypt and brought you into the land that I swore to give to your fathers."

Judg 13:17-18. Manoah said to the angel of the LORD, "What is your name, so that, when your words come true, we may honor you?" And the angel of the LORD said to him, "Why do you ask my name, seeing it is wonderful."

Gen 15:1. The word of the LORD came to Abram in a vision.

1 Sam 3:1, 10, 21. And the word of the LORD was rare in those days; there was no frequent vision. ... And the LORD came and stood, calling as at other times, "Samuel! Samuel!" ... And the LORD appeared again at Shiloh, for the LORD revealed himself to Samuel at Shiloh by the word of the LORD.

Isa 30:27-28. Behold, the name of the LORD comes from afar, burning with his anger, and in thick rising smoke; his lips are full of fury, and his tongue is like a devouring fire; his breath is like an overflowing stream that reaches up to the neck.

Jer 1:4, 9. Now the word of the LORD came to me ... then the LORD put out his hand and touched my mouth.

[b] **John 1:1-3, 14.** In the beginning was the Word, and the Word was with God, and the Word was God ... The Word became flesh and dwelt among us.

John 17:6, 11-12. "I have manifested your name to the people whom you gave me out of the world. ... Holy Father, keep them in your name, which you have given me, that they may be one, even as we are one.

Jude 5. Now I want to remind you, although you once fully knew it, that Jesus, who saved a people out of the land of Egypt, afterward destroyed those who did not believe.

Question 11. Why did God manifest himself as this angel?

Since the Father may not be seen,[a] the Angel of the LORD is God's visible messenger to humans.[b]

[a] **John 5:37.** The Father who sent me has himself borne witness about me. His voice you have never heard, his form you have never seen.

John 6:46. Not that anyone has seen the Father except he who is from God; he has seen the Father.

[b] **Gen 32:24, 27, 29-30.** And a man wrestled with [Jacob] until the breaking of the day ... and [the man] said to him, "What is your name?" And he said, "Jacob." ...

Then Jacob asked him, "Please tell me your name." But he said, "Why is it that you ask my name?" And there he blessed him. So Jacob called the name of the place Peniel, saying, "For I have seen God face to face, and yet my life has been delivered."

Exod 33:19-20. [The LORD said], "I will make all my goodness pass before you and will proclaim before you my name 'The LORD.' And I will be gracious to whom I will be gracious, and will show mercy on whom I will show mercy. But," he said, "you cannot see my face, for man shall not see me and live."

John 1:18. No one has ever seen God; the only God, who is at the Father's side, he has made him known.

Question 12. Did this Angel of the LORD have a beginning?

No, since the Old Testament's Angel of the LORD is identified as the LORD,[5] who has no beginning and no end.[a; 6]

a **Pss 90:1-2**. Lord ... Before the mountains were brought forth, or ever you had formed the earth and the world, from everlasting to everlasting you are God.

---

5. See question 10.

6. Note that Isa 9:6 is 9:5 MT. God's uncreated, incomparable nature is also known through his names. He is "everlasting Father" (*'abi'ad*; Isa 9:6), the "Ancient of Days" (*'attiq yomin*; Dan 7:9), the "everlasting God" (*'el 'olam*; Gen 21:33).

Jude 25. To the only God, our Savior, through Jesus Christ our Lord, be glory, majesty, dominion, and authority, before all time and now and forever. Amen.

PART 2

THE LESSER GODS

Question 13. What is *'elohim*?

'elohim is a Hebrew word which means "God" or "gods."

Question 14. Is God—that is, the God of Israel—an *'elohim*?

Yes, *'elohim* is a word that is very often used for God. The term is not used exclusively for God,[1] and so the term does not refer to God's unique nature or attributes.

Gen 1:1. In the beginning God (*'elohim*) created the heavens and the earth.

Gen 17:3 Then Abram fell on his face. And God (*'elohim*) said to him.

---

1. See questions 15 and 17.

Exod 2:24. God (*'elohim*) heard their groaning, and God remembered his covenant with Abraham, with Isaac, and with Jacob.

Question 15. If God and gods are all described with *'elohim*, then what do all gods (*'elohim*) have in common?

All gods are spirits (spiritual beings) whose domain is the spiritual world.[a; 2] All disembodied inhabitants of the spiritual world are, by definition, *'elohim*, since *'elohim* is a term used to identify spirit beings. Some spiritual beings exercise dominion and rule given to them by God; they act either in concert with his will or in rebellion.[b]

[a] **Pss 104:4** Who makes his angels spirits.

John 4:24. God is spirit.

Rev 16:14. They are demonic spirits.

---

2. The Hebrew Bible uses the word *'elohim*, the most common term for God, of other beings besides the God of Israel (e.g., Deut 32:17; Pss 82:1b; 1 Sam 28:13). See questions 16–17. Consequently, *'elohim* does not point to a specific set of attributes. Rather, it describes a resident of the spiritual world. Yahweh, the God of Israel, the first person of the Trinity, is an *'elohim*, but no other *'elohim* are Yahweh. The God of Israel is distinguished as unique and incomparable in other ways. See *The Unseen Realm*, Chapter 4.

[b] **Pss 82:1–2**. God has taken his place in the divine council; in the midst of the gods he holds judgment: "How long will you judge unjustly?"

Deut 32:8. When the Most High gave to the nations their inheritance, when he divided mankind, he fixed the borders of the peoples according to the number of the sons of God.[3]

Dan 5:21. The Most High God rules the kingdom of mankind and sets over it whom he will.

Dan 10:20. I will return to fight against the prince of Persia; and when I go out, behold, the prince of Greece will come.

Eph 6:12. We do not wrestle against flesh and blood, but against the rulers, against the authorities, against the cosmic powers over this present darkness, against the spiritual forces of evil in the heavenly places.

Question 16. Are there more gods (*'elohim*) than the One God of Israel?

There are many gods;[a] but the one true God is eternally the incomparable God.[b]

[a] **Exod 20:3**. You shall have no other gods before me.

---

3. ESV differs from most translations here but is correct. "Sons of God" is the reading of the oldest Hebrew texts, the Dead Sea Scrolls.

Deut 10:17. For the LORD your God is God of gods and Lord of lords, the great, the mighty, and the awesome God.

Deut 32:17 NASB. They sacrificed to demons who were not God, To gods whom they have not known.

Pss 138:1. I give you thanks, O LORD, with my whole heart; before the gods I sing your praise.

Pss 82:1. God has taken his place in the divine council; in the midst of the gods he holds judgment.

1 Cor 8:5. Although there may be so-called gods in heaven or on earth—as indeed there are many "gods."

2 Cor 4:4. The god of this world has blinded the minds of the unbelievers.

[b] **Neh 9:6.** "You are the LORD, you alone. You have made heaven, the heaven of heavens, with all their host, the earth and all that is on it, the seas and all that is in them; and you preserve all of them; and the host of heaven worships you."

Pss 86:8, 10. There is none like you among the gods, O Lord, nor are there any works like yours ... For you are great and do wondrous things; you alone are God.

Pss 95:3. For the LORD is a great God, and a great King above all gods.

Pss 136:2. Give thanks to the God of gods, for his steadfast love endures forever.

Isa 44:8. Is there a God besides me? There is no Rock; I know not any.[4]

Isa 45:5. I am the LORD, and there is no other, besides me there is no God.

Isa 45:21. And there is no other god besides me, a righteous God and a Savior; there is none besides me.

1 Cor 8:6. Yet for us there is one God, the Father, from whom are all things and for whom we exist, and one Lord, Jesus Christ, through whom are all things and through whom we exist.

Question 17. Who are these other gods?

These other gods are created spiritual beings, such as the sons of God, assigned to govern the nations when God judged the nations at Babel,[a; 5] demons,[b; 6] and the human dead.[c]

[a] **Pss 82:1, 6**. God has taken his place in the divine council; in the midst of the gods he holds judgment ... I said, "You are gods, sons of the Most High, all of you."

Deut 32:8. When the Most High gave to the nations their inheritance, when he divided mankind he fixed

---

4. See Deut 32:4, 31.

5. See question 33.

6. See question 74 on the difference between "demons" in the Old Testament and New Testament.

the borders of the peoples according to the number of the sons of God.[7]

Deut 32:43. "Rejoice with him, O heavens; bow down to him, all gods."

[b] **Deut 32:17** NASB. "They sacrificed to demons who were not God, To gods whom they have not known.

1 Cor 10:21-22 You cannot drink the cup of the Lord and the cup of demons. You cannot partake of the table of the Lord and the table of demons. Shall we provoke the Lord to jealousy? Are we stronger than he?[8]

[c] **1 Sam 28:13-14.** King [Saul] said to [the witch of Endor], "Do not be afraid. What do you see?" And the woman said to Saul, "I see a god coming up out of the earth." He said to her, "What is his appearance?" And she said, "An old man is coming up, and he is wrapped in a robe." And Saul knew that it was Samuel, and he bowed with his face to the ground and paid homage.

---

7. For the reading "sons of God," see page 17, footnote 3.
8. Paul is drawing upon Deut 32:17 for this statement.

Question 18. Should Christians affirm that there are more gods than one?

Yes, because all of these beings are described by the same Hebrew word, *'elohim*.[9] They each have real existence and are not mere idols; demons are not idols, nor do idols have access to God's council.[10] But none of these *'elohim* are comparable to God.[11]

> **Pss 40:5.** You have multiplied, O LORD my God, your wondrous deeds and your thoughts toward us; none can compare with you!

> **Isa 40:18.** To whom then will you liken God, or what likeness compare with him?

Question 19. What is meant by "God is eternally the uncomparable God"?[12]

God cannot be deposed or lose his right to rule; there never was and never will be a time when he was not absolutely Sovereign over all of his creation.

---

9. See the Scripture references in question 16-17. Each time "gods" appears in these verses, it is the word *'elohim*. The biblical writers use *'elohim* this way because it does not point to a specific set of attributes. Rather, it describes a resident of the spiritual world.

10. See Section IV. In the ancient world, idols were thought to *contain* spirits (*'elohim*) to localize a deity for worship and negotiation. When an idol was destroyed the *'elohim* was not thought of as dead, but in need of another host.

11. See the Scripture references in question 16.

12. See answer to question 16.

Isa 44:6. I am the first and I am the last; besides me there is no god.

Col 1:17. [Christ] is before all things, and in him all things hold together.

Rev 1:8. "I am the Alpha and the Omega," says the Lord God, "who is and who was and who is to come, the Almighty."

Rev 22:13. I [Jesus] am the Alpha and the Omega, the first and the last, the beginning and the end.

Question 20. If there are other gods, how can God be God alone?

By "God alone" we mean that God is not comparable with any part of his creation, including other spiritual beings who are created.[a] He is utterly distinct: He has no peer to his nature;[b] there is no rival to his throne;[c] there is no equal to his character;[d] there is no other universal sovereign king over all other gods.[e]

[a] **Pss 148:1–5**. Praise the LORD from the heavens; praise him in the heights! Praise him, all his angels; praise him, all his hosts! Praise him, sun and moon, praise him, all you shining stars! Praise him, you highest heavens, and you waters above the heavens! Let them praise the name of the LORD! For he commanded and they were created.

Neh 9:6. You are the LORD, you alone. You have made heaven, the heaven of heavens, with all their host, the earth and all that is on it, the seas and all that is in them; and you preserve all of them; and the host of heaven worships you.

Deut 4:19. And beware lest you raise your eyes to heaven, and when you see the sun and the moon and the stars, all the host of heaven, you be drawn away and bow down to them and serve them.

Deut 17:2-3. If there is found among you ... a man or woman who does what is evil in the sight of the LORD your God, in transgressing his covenant, and has gone and served other gods and worshiped them, or the sun or the moon or any of the host of heaven, which I have forbidden

Jas 1:17. Every good gift and every perfect gift is from above, coming down from the Father of lights with whom there is no variation or shadow due to change.[13]

b **Isa 44:8**. Is there a God besides me? There is no Rock; I know not any.

Isa 45:5. I am the LORD, and there is no other, besides me there is no God.

Mark 2:7. Who can forgive sins but God alone?

---

13. James calls God "the Father of lights," a phrase that points to God as the creator of celestial objects. The verse therefore declares that God is the creator of all heavenly beings since, like the cultures of the wider ancient world, the biblical writers conceived of the stars as heavenly beings (Job 38:7).

^c **Deut 33:26**. There is none like God, O Jeshurun, who rides through the heavens to your help, through the skies in his majesty.

Pss 113:5–6. Who is like the LORD our God, who is seated on high, who looks far down on the heavens and the earth?

^d **1 Kgs 8:23**. O LORD, God of Israel, there is no God like you, in heaven above or on earth beneath, keeping covenant and showing steadfast love to your servants who walk before you with all their heart.

Isa 45:21. And there is no other god besides me, a righteous God and a Savior; there is none besides me.

Mic 7:18. Who is a God like you, pardoning iniquity and passing over transgression for the remnant of his inheritance?

^e **Pss 95:3**. For the LORD is a great God, and a great King above all gods.

Pss 136:2. Give thanks to the God of gods, for his steadfast love endures forever.

Pss 29:1–2. Ascribe to the LORD, O heavenly beings, ascribe to the LORD glory and strength. Ascribe to the LORD the glory due his name; worship the LORD in the splendor of holiness.

Question 21. Was God ever like us?

While the Word and the Name made God visible to humans,[14] God was never like man or any of his creation either in nature[a] or character.[b] He has created man as his image,[c; 15] and through the incarnation as Jesus, added to himself our human nature,[d] in order to save us from our sins,[e] and restore us to a position of authority and dominion.[f; 16]

[a] **Exod 15:11**. Who is like you, O LORD, among the gods? Who is like you, majestic in holiness, awesome in glorious deeds, doing wonders?

Isa 44:7. Who is like me? Let him proclaim it. Let him declare and set it before me, since I appointed an ancient people. Let them declare what is to come, and what will happen.

[b] **Num 23:19**. God is not man, that he should lie, or a son of man, that he should change his mind.

1 Sam 15:29. The Glory of Israel will not lie or have regret, for he is not a man, that he should have regret.

[c] **Gen 1:26–27**. Then God said, "Let us make man in our image, after our likeness. And let them have dominion

---

14. See question 11.

15. See *The Unseen Realm*, Chapters 7–9.

16. The idea of restoring humanity's position of authority and dominion is a major theme that will be taken up later. See Section IV.

over the fish of the sea and over the birds of the heavens and over the livestock and over all the earth and over every creeping thing that creeps on the earth." So God created man in his own image, in the image of God he created him; male and female he created them.

d **Luke 1:35.** The angel answered [Mary], "The Holy Spirit will come upon you, and the power of the Most High will overshadow you; therefore the child to be born will be called holy—the Son of God."

John 1:14. The Word became flesh and dwelt among us.

1 Cor 15:47. The first man was from the earth, a man of dust; the second man is from heaven.

Phil 2:5-7. Christ Jesus, who, though he was in the form of God, did not count equality with God a thing to be grasped, but emptied himself, by taking the form of a servant, being born in the likeness of men.

e **Matt 1:21.** You shall call his name Jesus, for he will save his people from their sins.

Titus 2:14. [Jesus] gave himself for us to redeem us from all lawlessness and to purify for himself a people for his own possession who are zealous for good works.

Heb 7:25. [Jesus] is able to save to the uttermost those who draw near to God through him.

1 John 1:7. The blood of Jesus his Son cleanses us from all sin.

f **Matt 16:19.** I will give you the keys of the kingdom of heaven, and whatever you bind on earth shall be bound in heaven, and whatever you loose on earth shall be loosed in heaven.

Matt 28:18–19. All authority in heaven and on earth has been given to me. Go therefore and make disciples of all nations.

Titus 2:15. Declare these things; exhort and rebuke with all authority.

PART 3

THE SONS OF GOD

Question 22. Does God have more sons than *the* Son of God (Jesus)?

Yes, God has other sons in heaven and on earth.

> **Exod 4:22** NASB. Israel is My son, My firstborn.

> **Job 1:6.** Now there was a day when the sons of God came to present themselves before the LORD.

> **Job 38:7.** [Where were you] when the morning stars sang together and all the sons of God shouted for joy?

> **Acts 17:29.** Being then God's offspring, we ought not to think that the divine being is like gold or silver or stone.

> **Gal 3:26.** In Christ Jesus you are all sons of God, through faith.

Question 23. Who are these other sons?

God's heavenly sons are called the sons of God,[a] and his earthly sons are humankind.[b]

[a] **Gen 6:2**. The sons of God saw that the daughters of man were attractive. And they took as their wives any they chose.

Job 1:6. Now there was a day when the sons of God came to present themselves before the LORD.

Job 2:1. Again there was a day when the sons of God came to present themselves before the LORD.

Job 38:7. [Where were you] when the morning stars sang together and all the sons of God shouted for joy?

Deut 32:8. When the Most High gave to the nations their inheritance, when he divided mankind, he fixed the borders of the peoples according to the number of the sons of God.[1]

Pss 29:1. Ascribe to the LORD, O heavenly beings,[2] ascribe to the LORD glory and strength.

Pss 82:6. I said, "You are gods, sons of the Most High, all of you."

---

1. For the reading "sons of God," see page 17, footnote 3.

2. "Heavenly beings" is *bney 'elim* in Hebrew. *'Elim* is the plural of *'El*. *Bney 'elim* is literally "sons of God(s)." The same phrase occurs in Psa 89:6.

Pss 89:6. For who in the skies can be compared to the Lord? Who among the heavenly beings is like the Lord?

b **Exod 4:22** NASB. Israel is My son, My first-born.

Hos 11:1. When Israel was a child, I loved him, and out of Egypt I called my son.

Luke 3:38. [Jesus,] the son of Enosh, the son of Seth, the son of Adam, the son of God.

Acts 17:29. Being then God's offspring, we ought not to think that the divine being is like gold or silver or stone.

Rom 8:14. For all who are led by the Spirit of God are sons of God.

Gal 3:26. For in Christ Jesus you are all sons of God, through faith.

Question 24. How do all other sons of God differ from Jesus, the Son of God?

Jesus Christ is the unique Son of God, very God of very God, *begotten* but uncreated.[3]

a **John 1:18** NASB. No one has seen God at any time; the only begotten God who is in the bosom of the Father, He has explained *Him*.

---

3. See *The Unseen Realm*, Chapters 4 and 36.

John 3:16 NASB. For God so loved the world, that He gave His only begotten Son, that whoever believes in Him should not perish, but have eternal life.

1 John 4:9 NASB. God has sent His only begotten Son into the world.

Question 25. What does "begotten" mean?

"Begotten" means "unique" or "one of a kind."[4]

Heb 11:17 NASB. By faith Abraham, when he was tested, offered up Isaac; and he who had received the promises was offering up his only begotten *son*.[5]

Question 26. How does the designation "sons of God" differ from "'elohim" or "angel"?

All disembodied spirit beings are *'elohim*. "Angel" is a designation of function—angels are messengers, and may or may not be sons of God. "Sons of God" is a term of high rank in God's spiritual hierarchy; it denotes administrative tasks of greater significance (territorial rulership, decision-making status in the divine council).

---

4. The Greek word in Heb 11:17 is *monogenēs*. It is the same word as found in John 1:18; 3:16; 1 John 4:9.

5. The verse indicates that "begotten" (*monogenēs*) cannot mean "only one, period," since Isaac was not even Abraham's firstborn son. That privilege belonged to Ishmael. Rather, Isaac was the *unique* son (the son of the promise, the son of the miracle birth).

Question 27. What other terms describe the heavenly sons of God?

The heavenly sons of God are described with many terms, among them watchers,[a] the hosts of heaven,[b] the divine council,[c] rulers or princes,[d] cosmic powers or authorities,[e] lords,[f] thrones or dominions,[g] archangels,[h] and glorious ones.[i]

[a] **Dan 4:13.** I saw in the visions of my head as I lay in bed, and behold, a watcher, a holy one, came down from heaven.

Dan 4:17. The sentence is by the decree of the watchers, the decision by the word of the holy ones, to the end that the living may know that the Most High rules the kingdom of men.

[b] **1 Kgs 22:19–21.** And Micaiah said, "Therefore hear the word of the LORD: I saw the LORD sitting on his throne, and all the host of heaven standing beside him on his right hand and on his left; and the LORD said, 'Who will entice Ahab, that he may go up and fall at Ramoth-gilead?' And one said one thing, and another said another. Then a spirit came forward and stood before the LORD, saying, 'I will entice him.' "

[c] **Pss 82:1, 6.** God has taken his place in the divine council; in the midst of the gods he holds judgment. ... You are gods, sons of the Most High, all of you.

^d **Eph 2:1-2.** And you were dead in the trespasses and sins in which you once walked, following the course of this world, following the prince of the power of the air.

1 Cor 2:7-8. We impart a secret and hidden wisdom of God, which God decreed before the ages for our glory. None of the rulers of this age understood this, for if they had, they would not have crucified the Lord of glory.

Dan 10:13. The prince of the kingdom of Persia withstood [the angel Gabriel] twenty-one days, but Michael, one of the chief princes, came to help me, for I was left there with the kings of Persia.

^e **Eph 3:10**. Through the church the manifold wisdom of God might now be made known to the rulers and authorities in the heavenly places.

Eph 6:12. For we do not wrestle against flesh and blood, but against the rulers, against the authorities, against the cosmic powers over this present darkness, against the spiritual forces of evil in the heavenly places.

Rom 8:38-39. For I am sure that neither death nor life, nor angels nor rulers, nor things present nor things to come, nor powers ... will be able to separate us from the love of God.

^f **1 Cor 8:5**. Indeed there are many "gods" and many "lords."

g **Col 1:16**. For by him all things were created, in heaven and on earth, visible and invisible, whether thrones or dominions or rulers or authorities—all things were created through him and for him.

h **1 Thess 4:16**. For the Lord himself will descend from heaven with a cry of command, with the voice of an archangel, and with the sound of the trumpet of God. And the dead in Christ will rise first.

Jude 9. But when the archangel Michael, contending with the devil.

i **2 Pet 2:10–11**. Bold and willful, they do not tremble as they blaspheme the glorious ones, whereas angels, though greater in might and power, do not pronounce a blasphemous judgment against them before the Lord.

Question 28. What are seraphim?

Seraphim are shining divine beings who guard the throne of God; their appearance also includes serpentine and human features as well as wings.[6]

---

6. The description of the *seraphim* is drawn from Egyptian throne iconography due to the Egyptian context of the rule of Uzziah, Ahaz, and Hezekiah. The term comes from Hebrew *saraph* and Egyptian *seraf*. In terms of function, seraphim and cherubim are interchangeable (throne guardians). This is clearly shown in the ark of the covenant (Exod 25:22), where a Babylonian term (*cherubim*) is used to describe guardians of the divine presence in a way that other cherubim (Ezek 1,10) are

Num 21:6-7. The LORD sent fiery (*seraph*) serpents among the people, and they bit the people ... and the people came to Moses and said ... "take away the serpents (*nahash*) from us.

Isa 6:2-3. Above him stood the seraphim. Each had six wings: with two he covered his face, and with two he covered his feet, and with two he flew. And one called to another and said: "Holy, holy, holy is the LORD of hosts; the whole earth is full of his glory!"

Question 29. What are cherubim?

Cherubim are shining divine beings who guard the throne of God; their appearance is partly human and partly animal.[7]

Gen 3:24. [God] placed the cherubim and a flaming sword that turned every way to guard the way to the tree of life.

---

not. The context of the ark and the exodus is Egyptian. See *The Unseen Realm*, Chapters 10 and 34.

7. The description of cherubim is drawn from Akkadian/Babylonian throne iconography due to the historical Babylonian context of Ezekiel and the Mesopotamian literary context of the Eden story. The term comes from Akkadian/Babylonian *karibu*. In terms of function, seraphim and cherubim are interchangeable (throne guardians). See *The Unseen Realm*, Chapters 10 and 34.

Exod 25:22. I will meet with you, and from above the mercy seat, from between the two cherubim that are on the ark of the testimony

Ezek 1:4-8, 13-14, 22, 26. As I looked, behold, a stormy wind came out of the north, and a great cloud, with brightness around it, and fire flashing forth continually, and in the midst of the fire, as it were gleaming metal. And from the midst of it came the likeness of four living creatures. And this was their appearance: they had a human likeness, but each had four faces, and each of them had four wings. Their legs were straight, and the soles of their feet were like the sole of a calf's foot. And they sparkled like burnished bronze. Under their wings on their four sides they had human hands. ... As for the likeness of the living creatures, their appearance was like burning coals of fire, like the appearance of torches moving to and fro among the living creatures. And the fire was bright, and out of the fire went forth lightning. And the living creatures darted to and fro, like the appearance of a flash of lightning. ... Over the heads of the living creatures there was the likeness of an expanse, shining like awe-inspiring crystal, spread out above their heads. ... And above the expanse over their heads there was the likeness of a throne, in appearance like sapphire; and seated above the likeness of a throne was a likeness with a human appearance.

Ezek 28:13-14. You were in Eden, the garden of God; every precious stone was your covering ... You were an anointed guardian cherub. I placed you; you were on the holy mountain of God; in the midst of the stones of fire you walked.

Question 30. Are cherubim and seraphim *'elohim*?

Cherubim and seraphim are spirit beings, and so they are *'elohim* along with all other spirit beings.[8] Their function as throne guardians sets them apart from other *'elohim.*[9]

Question 31. Why do the sons of God have so many titles of authority?

The titles of the sons of God reflect their position of authority. Because God is the king and they are his sons, God gave them subservient rule as princes over smaller, earthly kingdoms as their inheritance.[10]

Deut 32:7-9. Remember the days of old; consider the years of many generations; ask your father, and he will show you, your elders, and they will tell you. When the Most High gave to the nations their inheritance, when he divided mankind, he fixed the borders of the peoples according to the number of the sons of God. But

---

8. See question 15 and 17.
9. See questions 28 and 29.
10. See questions 21 and 32.

the LORD's portion is his people, Jacob his allotted heritage.

Dan 10:13, 20. The prince of the kingdom of Persia withstood me twenty-one days, but Michael, one of the chief princes, came to help me, for I was left there with the kings of Persia ... Do you know why I have come to you? But now I will return to fight against the prince of Persia; and when I go out, behold, the prince of Greece will come.

Dan 12:1. At that time shall arise Michael, the great prince who has charge of your people.

Question 32. Do the earthly sons of God share the same kind of authority?

Yes, God created man to mirror the heavenly dominion on earth;[a; 11] this dominion has expressed itself through physical earthly kingdoms[b] and through the kingdom of Christ.[c; 12]

[a] **Gen 10:1ff.** There are the generations of the sons of Noah, Shem, Ham, and Japheth. Sons were born to them after the flood. (From here, the rest of the chapter gives 70 descendants of the sons of Noah).

Deut 32:8. When the Most High gave to the nations their inheritance, when he divided mankind, he fixed

---

11. See question 21 for the basis of humanity's dominion.
12. See *The Unseen Realm*, Chapters 34–36, 42.

the borders of the peoples according to the number [seventy] of the sons of God.[13] (There are seventy nations listed in the Table of Nations in Gen 10.)

Exod 24:1. Come up to the LORD, you and Aaron, Nadab, and Abihu, and seventy of the elders of Israel, and worship from afar.

Luke 10:1, 17 NASB. Now after this the Lord appointed seventy others, and sent them in pairs ahead of Him to every city and place where He Himself was going to come. ... The seventy returned with joy, saying, "Lord, even the demons are subject to us in Your name."

[b] **Dan 4:36.** At the same time my reason returned to me, and for the glory of my kingdom, my majesty and splendor returned to me. My counselors and my lords sought me, and I was established in my kingdom, and still more greatness was added to me.

[c] **Dan 4:34-35.** At the end of the days I, Nebuchadnezzar, lifted my eyes to heaven, and my reason returned to me, and I blessed the Most High, and praised and honored him who lives forever, for his dominion is an everlasting dominion, and his kingdom endures from generation to generation; all the inhabitants of the earth are accounted as nothing, and he does according to his will among the host of heaven and among the inhabitants

---

13. For the reading "sons of God," see page 17, footnote 3.

of the earth; and none can stay his hand or say to him, "What have you done?"

Matt 12:28. If it is by the Spirit of God that I cast out demons, then the kingdom of God has come upon you.

PART 4

DIVINE COUNCIL

Question 33. When did the heavenly sons of God receive their authority to rule?

The sons of God were part of God's rule in the invisible spiritual realm before the creation of the visible heavens and earth.[a] After Adam, the human son of God, abdicated his earthly authority and after the rebellion of the human survivors of the flood at the Tower of Babel, the heavenly sons of God were allotted nations to rule over.[b]

[a] **Job 38:6-7**. On what were [the] bases [of the earth] sunk, or who laid its cornerstone, when the morning stars sang together and all the sons of God shouted for joy?

[b] **Deut 32:7-8**. Remember the days of old; consider the years of many generations; ask your father, and he will show you, your elders, and they will tell you. When the

Most High gave to the nations their inheritance, when he divided mankind, he fixed the borders of the peoples according to the number of the sons of God.[1]

Question 34. Did the heavenly sons of God rule well?

No, the sons of God did not rule well. They ruled in wickedness and deceived the nations,[a] keeping them in ignorance of the true God.[b] God announced in council that they are destined for judgment.[c]

[a] **Deut 4:19** And beware lest you raise your eyes to heaven, and when you see the sun and the moon and the stars, all the host of heaven, you be drawn away and bow down to them and serve them, things that the LORD your God has allotted to all the peoples under the whole heaven.[2]

Deut 32:8. When the Most High gave to the nations their inheritance, when he divided mankind, he fixed the borders of the peoples according to the number of the sons of God.

Deut 29:26. [They] went and served other gods and worshiped them, gods whom they had not known and whom he had not allotted to them.

---

1. For the reading "sons of God," see page 17, footnote 3.
2. See *The Unseen Realm*, Chapters 14–15.

Pss 82:1-4. God has taken his place in the divine council; in the midst of the gods he holds judgment: "How long will you judge unjustly and show partiality to the wicked? Give justice to the weak and the fatherless; maintain the right of the afflicted and the destitute. Rescue the weak and the needy; deliver them from the hand of the wicked."

b **Acts 7:42**. But God turned away and gave them over to worship the host of heaven.

Acts 17:26-27. He made from one man every nation of mankind to live on all the face of the earth, having determined allotted periods and the boundaries of their dwelling place, that they should seek God, in the hope that they might feel their way toward him and find him.

c **Pss 82:6-8**. You are gods, sons of the Most High, all of you; nevertheless, like men you shall die, and fall like any prince. Arise, O God, judge the earth; for you shall inherit all the nations!

Isa 24:21. On that day the LORD will punish the host of heaven, in heaven, and the kings of the earth, on the earth.

Isa 34:2, 4. For the LORD is enraged against all the nations, and furious against all their host; he has devoted them to destruction, has given them over for slaughter. ... All the host of heaven shall rot away, and the skies roll up like a scroll. All their host hall fall, as leaves fall from the vine, like leaves falling from the fig tree.

Question 35. Did the heavenly sons of God ruin God's good plan for humanity by keeping the entire world ignorant of God?

Although the whole earth was deceived,[a] God created a new people through Abraham[b] and took them for himself as an inheritance.[c] From them he brought forth the Son to save his children who trust in him.[d]

[a] **John 12:46**. I have come into the world as light, so that whoever believes in me may not remain in darkness.

Eph 2:1-2. And you were dead in the trespasses and sins in which you once walked, following the course of this world, following the prince of the power of the air, the spirit that is now at work in the sons of disobedience.

[b] **Gen 22:18**. In [Abraham's] offspring shall all the nations of the earth be blessed.

[c] **Deut 32:8-9**. When the Most High gave to the nations their inheritance, when he divided mankind, he fixed the borders of the peoples according to the number of the sons of God. But the LORD's portion is his people, Jacob his allotted heritage.

Deut 7:6. For you are a people holy to the LORD your God. The LORD your God has chosen you to be a people for his treasured possession, out of all the peoples who are on the face of the earth.

Pss 2:7–8. I will tell of the decree: The LORD said to me, "You are my Son; today I have begotten you. Ask of me, and I will make the nations your heritage, and the ends of the earth your possession.

d **Heb 1:2**. In these last days he has spoken to us by his Son, whom he appointed the heir of all things.

Gal 3:26–29. For in Christ Jesus you are all sons of God, through faith. For as many of you as were baptized into Christ have put on Christ. There is neither Jew nor Greek, there is neither slave nor free, there is no male and female, for you are all one in Christ Jesus. And if you are Christ's, then you are Abraham's offspring, heirs according to promise.

Question 36. What is the divine council?

The divine council is the assembly of the heavenly sons of God, the divine beings who administer the affairs of the cosmos.

Pss 82:1. God has taken his place in the divine council; in the midst of the gods he holds judgment.

Pss 89:6–7. For who in the skies can be compared to the LORD? Who among the heavenly beings is like the LORD, a God greatly to be feared in the council of the holy ones, and awesome above all who are around him?

1 Kgs 22:19–21. And Micaiah said, "Therefore hear the word of the LORD: I saw the LORD sitting on his throne, and all the host of heaven standing beside him on his right hand and on his left; and the LORD said, 'Who will entice Ahab, that he may go up and fall at Ramoth-gilead?' And one said one thing, and another said another. Then a spirit came forward and stood before the LORD, saying, 'I will entice him.' "

Dan 4:17. The sentence is by the decree of the watchers, the decision by the word of the holy ones.

Dan 7:9. As I looked, thrones were placed, and the Ancient of Days took his seat; his clothing was white as snow, and the hair of his head like pure wool; his throne was fiery flames; its wheels were burning fire.

Question 37. Where does the divine council meet?

The divine council meets in the abode and presence of God. This abode is described as being in the heavens, on a well-watered, cosmic garden, or a lofty mountain, far removed on high, as those places are the home of God in Scripture.[3]

> **Gen 28:12-13, 17** And [Jacob] dreamed, and behold, there was a ladder set up on the earth, and the top of it reached to heaven. And behold, the angels of God were ascending and descending on it! And behold, the

---

3. Note that the decorations of the temple are filled with garden imagery (1 Kgs 6–7; Ezek 40:2, 31–34; 41:17–20; 47:1–12). Tent imagery (e.g., the tabernacle and the tent within the sanctuary of the temple) is also familiar divine abode imagery in the ancient Near East. See *The Unseen Realm*, Chapters 6 and 26.

L<small>ORD</small> stood above it and said, "I am the L<small>ORD</small>, the God of Abraham your father and the God of Isaac. ... And [Jacob] was afraid and said, "How awesome is this place! This is none other than the house of God, and this is the gate of heaven."

Exod 24:9-10. Then Moses and Aaron, Nadab, and Abihu, and seventy of the elders of Israel went up [onto Mount Sinai], and they saw the God of Israel. There was under his feet as it were a pavement of sapphire stone, like the very heaven for clearness.

Isa 14:13. You said in your heart, 'I will ascend to heaven; above the stars of God I will set my throne on high; I will sit on the mount of assembly in the far reaches of the north.

Isa 33:20. Behold, Zion, the city of our appointed feasts! ... there the L<small>ORD</small> in Majesty will be for us a place of broad rivers and streams.

Ezek 28:2, 13-14. Thus says the Lord G<small>OD</small>: "Because your heart is proud, and you have said, 'I am a god, I sit in the seat of the gods, in the heart of the seas,' ... You were in Eden, the garden of God ... You were an anointed guardian cherub. I placed you; you were on the holy mountain of God; in the midst of the stones of fire you walked.

Pss 3:4 N<small>ASB</small>. I was crying to the L<small>ORD</small> with my voice, and He answered me from His holy mountain.

Pss 48:1–2. Great is the LORD and greatly to be praised in the city of our God! His holy mountain, beautiful in elevation, is the joy of all the earth, Mount Zion, in the far north, the city of the great King.

Question 38. Are all members of the divine council fallen and evil?

The LORD has those in heaven who remain faithful to him,[a] but many of high rank (that is, sons of God) rebelled against him.[b]

[a] **Josh 5:13–15** NASB. Now it came about when Joshua was by Jericho, that he lifted up his eyes and looked, and behold, a man was standing opposite him with his sword drawn in his hand, and Joshua went to him and said to him, "Are you for us or for our adversaries?" And he said, "No, rather I indeed come now *as* captain of the host of the LORD." And Joshua fell on his face to the earth, and bowed down, and said to him, "What has my lord to say to his servant?" And the captain of the LORD's host said to Joshua, "Remove your sandals from your feet, for the place where you are standing is holy." And Joshua did so.

1 Kgs 22:19–21. And Micaiah said, "Therefore hear the word of the LORD: I saw the LORD sitting on his throne, and all the host of heaven standing beside him on his right hand and on his left; and the LORD said, 'Who will entice Ahab, that he may go up and fall at Ramoth-gilead?' And one said one thing, and another said another. Then a spirit came forward and stood before the LORD, saying, 'I will entice him.' "

Pss 89:6-7. For who in the skies can be compared to the LORD? Who among the heavenly beings is like the LORD, a God greatly to be feared in the council of the holy ones?[4]

Dan 10:13. The prince of the kingdom of Persia withstood me [Gabriel the angel] twenty-one days, but Michael, one of the chief princes, came to help me, for I was left there with the kings of Persia.

Zech 14:4-5. On that day his feet shall stand on the Mount of Olives that lies before Jerusalem. ... Then the LORD my God will come, and all the holy ones with him.

Matt 4:11. Then the devil left him, and behold, angels came and were ministering to him.

Matt 16:27. For the Son of Man is going to come with his angels in the glory of his Father.

Luke 2:13-14. And suddenly there was with the angel a multitude of the heavenly host praising God and saying, "Glory to God in the highest, and on earth peace among those with whom he is pleased!"

1 Tim 5:21. ... the elect angels.

---

4. "Heavenly beings" is *bney 'elim* in Hebrew. *'Elim* is the plural of *'El*. *Bney 'elim* is literally "sons of God(s)." The same phrase occurs in Psa 89:6.

^b **Job 15:15**. Behold, God puts no trust in his holy ones, and the heavens are not pure in his sight.

Pss 82:1-2, 6-8. God has taken his place in the divine council; in the midst of the gods he holds judgment: "How long will you judge unjustly and show partiality to the wicked? ... You are gods, sons of the Most High, all of you; nevertheless, like men you shall die, and fall like any prince. Arise, O God, judge the earth; for you shall inherit all the nations!"

Dan 10:13. The prince of the kingdom of Persia withstood me twenty-one days, but Michael, one of the chief princes, came to help me, for I was left there with the kings of Persia.

Dan 10:20. But now I will return to fight against the prince of Persia; and when I go out, behold, the prince of Greece will come.

Isa 14:13. You said in your heart, "I will ascend to heaven; above the stars of God I will set my throne on high; I will sit on the mount of assembly in the far reaches of the north."

Ezek 28:2, 13-14. Thus says the Lord GOD: "Because your heart is proud, and you have said, 'I am a god, I sit in the seat of the gods, in the heart of the seas' ... You were in Eden, the garden of God ... You were an anointed guardian cherub. I placed you; you were on the holy mountain of God; in the midst of the stones of fire you walked."

Question 39. Who is the leader of the divine council?

The divine council is led by God himself, who is known by many names: El,[a] the Ancient of Days,[b] the Uncreated Creator who is the Name,[5] the same God incarnate in Jesus of Nazareth.[c]

[a] **Isa 14:13.** You said in your heart, "I will ascend to heaven; above the stars of God[6] I will set my throne on high; I will sit on the mount of assembly in the far reaches of the north."

Ezek 28:2. Son of man, say to the prince of Tyre, Thus says the Lord GOD [*Adonai Yahweh*]: "Because your heart is proud, and you have said, 'I am a god ['*el*], I sit in the seat of the gods ['*elohim*], in the heart of the seas.'"

[b] **Dan 7:9.** As I looked, thrones were placed, and the Ancient of Days took his seat; his clothing was white as snow, and the hair of his head like pure wool; his throne was fiery flames; its wheels were burning fire.

---

5. See question 10.

6. "God" translates the Hebrew word '*el* ("El") here. El is another name in the Hebrew Bible for Yahweh: "LORD, God Most High" = Yahweh El-Elyon (Gen 14:22); "The LORD (Yahweh) appeared to Abram and said to him, 'I am God Almighty (El-Shaddai)'" (Gen 17:1); "Who is God (El), but the LORD (Yahweh)?" (2 Sam 22:32).

c **John 1:1–3, 14.** In the beginning was the Word, and the Word was with God, and the Word was God ... The Word became flesh and dwelt among us.

John 17:6, 11. "I have manifested your name to the people whom you gave me out of the world. ... Holy Father, keep them in your name, which you have given me, that they may be one, even as we are one."

Jude 5. Now I want to remind you, although you once fully knew it, that Jesus, who saved a people out of the land of Egypt, afterward destroyed those who did not believe.

Question 40. What is the relationship of the Son of Man to the divine council?

The Son of Man is distinct from the Ancient of Days, who is Yahweh,[a] yet of the same divine essence, as he is described as coming upon/with the clouds, a description used only of Yahweh elsewhere in the Old Testament,[b] and is given everlasting rule over all nations, a description used of the Son, the second person of the Holy Trinity,[c] who rules from God's right hand, exalted above all powers, visible and invisible.[d]

a **Dan 7:9, 13.** As I looked, thrones were placed, and the Ancient of Days took his seat; his clothing was white as snow, and the hair of his head like pure wool; his throne was fiery flames; its wheels were burning fire.[7] ... I saw in the night visions, and behold, with the clouds of heaven there came one like a son of man, and he came to the Ancient of Days and was presented before him.

[b] **Deut 33:26**. There is none like God, O Jeshurun, who rides through the heavens to your help, through the skies in his majesty.

Pss 68:32–33. Sing to God; sing praises to the Lord, *Selah*, to him who rides in the heavens, the ancient heavens; behold, he sends out his voice, his mighty voice.

Pss 104:3. [The LORD] lays the beams of his chambers on the waters; he makes the clouds his chariot; he rides on the wings of the wind.

Isa 19:1. Behold, the LORD is riding on a swift cloud and comes to Egypt.

[c] **Dan 7:14**. And to him was given dominion and glory and a kingdom, that all peoples, nations, and languages should serve him; his dominion is an everlasting dominion, which shall not pass away, and his kingdom one that shall not be destroyed.

Matt 26:64. Jesus said to [Caiaphas], "You have said so. But I tell you, from now on you will see the Son of Man

---

7. Compare Ezek 1:16–28; 10:2.

seated at the right hand of Power and coming on the clouds of heaven."

Matt 28:18-20. Jesus came and said to them, "All authority in heaven and on earth has been given to me. Go therefore and make disciples of all nations, baptizing them in the name of the Father and of the Son and of the Holy Spirit, teaching them to observe all that I have commanded you. And behold, I am with you always, to the end of the age."

d **Eph 1:20-24.** [The Heavenly Father] seated [Christ] at his right hand in the heavenly places, far above all rule and authority and power and dominion, and above every name that is named, not only in this age but also in the one to come. And he put all things under his feet and gave him as head over all things to the church, which is his body, the fullness of him who fills all in all.

Phil 2:8-11. And being found in human form, he humbled himself by becoming obedient to the point of death, even death on a cross. Therefore God has highly exalted him and bestowed on him the name that is above every name, so that at the name of Jesus every knee should bow, in heaven and on earth and under the earth, and every tongue confess that Jesus Christ is Lord, to the glory of God the Father.

1 Pet 3:22. [Jesus Christ] has gone into heaven and is at the right hand of God, with angels, authorities, and powers having been subjected to him.

Rev 11:15. The kingdom of the world has become the kingdom of our Lord and of his Christ, and he shall reign forever and ever.

Question 41. What is the relationship of the Son of Man to the Angel of the LORD?

The Son of Man and the Angel of the Lord are the same second Person of the Holy Trinity. The Angel of the Lord is Yahweh, since the Name—who is Yahweh—indwells him.[a; 8] But the Angel of the Lord is also the the pre-incarnate embodiment of Yahweh, a messenger of and thus distinct from Yahweh.[b] Jesus is described as the incarnate Name,[c; 9] and is identified with the Angel as the One who saved Israel from Egypt.[d] The eschatological (OT) Son of Man, to whom an everlasting kingdom is given by the Ancient of Days, is Jesus.[e; 10] Therefore, Jesus, the Son of Man, is the incarnate Yahweh.

[a] **Exod 3:2, 4, 13-14.** The angel of the Lord appeared to [Moses] in a flame of fire out of the midst of a bush. ... When the Lord saw that [Moses] turned aside to see, God called to him out of the bush. ... Then Moses said to God, "If I come to the people of Israel and say to them, 'The God of your fathers has sent me to you,' and they ask me, 'What is his name?' what shall I say to them?"

---

8. See questions 10-12.

9. See question 10.

10. See question 40.

God said to Moses, "I am who I am." And he said, "Say this to the people of Israel, 'I am has sent me to you.'"

Exod 23:20–21. Behold, I send an angel before you to guard you on the way and to bring you to the place that I have prepared. Pay careful attention to him and obey his voice; do not rebel against him, for he will not pardon your transgression, for my name is in him.

b **Gen 19:24**. Then the LORD rained on Sodom and Gomorrah sulfur and fire from the LORD out of heaven.

c **John 17:6, 11–12**. I have manifested your name to the people whom you gave me out of the world. ... Holy Father, keep them in your name, which you have given me, that they may be one, even as we are one.

d **Deut 4:37**. [God] brought you out of Egypt with his own presence, by his great power.

Judg 2:1. Now the angel of the Lord went up from Gilgal to Bochim. And he said, "I brought you up from Egypt and brought you into the land that I swore to give to your fathers."

Jude 5. Now I want to remind you, although you once fully knew it, that Jesus, who saved a people out of the land of Egypt, afterward destroyed those who did not believe.

e **Dan 7:13**. I saw in the night visions, and behold, with the clouds of heaven there came one like a son of man.

Matt 24:30. Then will appear in heaven the sign of the Son of Man, and then all the tribes of the earth will mourn, and they will see the Son of Man coming on the clouds of heaven with power and great glory (cf. Mark 14:62).

PART 5

SIN, REBELLION, AND THE FALL

Question 42. Who is Adam?

Adam is the first man,[a] created in the image of God,[b; 1] placed in the cosmic garden / mountain,[c; 2] and given dominion and authority over the creatures of the earth.[d]

a **Gen 2:7.** The LORD God formed the man ['adam] of dust from the ground and breathed into his nostrils the breath of life, and the man became a living creature.

b **Gen 1:26–27.** Then God said, "Let us make man in our image, after our likeness." ... So God created man in his

---

1. See question 21.
2. See question 37.

own image, in the image of God he created him; male and female he created them.

c **Gen 2:8**. The LORD God planted a garden in Eden, in the east, and there he put the man whom he had formed.

Ezek 28:13-14. Eden, the garden of God ... the holy mountain of God.

d **Gen 1:26**. Let them have dominion over the fish of the sea and over the birds of the heavens and over the livestock and over all the earth and over every creeping thing that creeps on the earth.

Question 43. What does it mean to be created in the image of God?

The image of God means that God created humans to be his representative (his image) on earth.[3] As such, human life is sacred and has an exalted status over the rest of creation. In order to represent God, humans must share God's communicable attributes. Before the Fall, Adam represented God's freedom, holiness, knowledge, and authority, as God designed. The perfect image of God is seen in Jesus Christ, the second Adam.

2 Cor 4:4. Christ, who is the image of God.

---

3. See *The Unseen Realm*, Chapter 5.

Col 1:15. He is the image of the invisible God, the first-born of all creation.

Heb 1:3. [Christ] is the radiance of the glory of God and the exact imprint of his nature.

Question 44. Did humanity cease imaging God after the fall?

Our status as God's earthly representatives was not lost, though our ability to represent God though our ability to represent God was severely corrupted. Being holy as he is holy, having our mind captive to God, using our freedom to make decisions, and exercising dominion on the earth under his headship can only be fully realized through redemption and sanctification by conforming us to the perfect imager, his Son, Jesus Christ.

Eph 4:24. Put on the new self, created after the likeness of God in true righteousness and holiness.

Col 3:10. Put on the new self, which is being renewed in knowledge after the image of its creator.

Rom 8:29. For those whom he foreknew he also predestined to be conformed to the image of his Son.

1 Cor 15:49. Just as we have borne the image of the man of dust, we shall also bear the image of the man of heaven.

2 Cor 3:17-18. Now the Lord is the Spirit, and where the Spirit of the Lord is, there is freedom. And we all, with unveiled face, beholding the glory of the Lord, are being transformed into the same image from one degree of glory to another.

Phil 2:5. Have this mind among yourselves, which is yours in Christ Jesus.

Heb 1:3. [Jesus] is the radiance of the glory of God and the exact imprint of his nature.

John 3:2. Beloved, we are God's children now, and what we will be has not yet appeared; but we know that when he appears we shall be like him, because we shall see him as he is.

Question 45. How was Adam's dominion to be carried out?

Adam was to carry out dominion as God's truth-speaker (prophet),[a] as the keeper of God's cosmic garden / mountain sanctuary (priest),[b] and as God's co-regent (king) over the physical creation.[c] Jesus, the second Adam, was God's sinless prophet, priest, and king, the full expression of what it means to image God.

[a] **Gen 3:2-3.** The woman said to the serpent, "We may eat of the fruit of the trees in the garden, but God said, 'You shall not eat of the fruit of the tree that is in the midst of the garden, neither shall you touch it, lest you die.'"

[b] **Gen 2:15.** The LORD God took the man and put him in the garden of Eden to work it and keep it.[4]

[c] **Gen 1:28.** And God blessed them. And God said to them, "Be fruitful and multiply and fill the earth and subdue it, and have dominion over the fish of the sea and over the birds of the heavens and over every living thing that moves on the earth."

Gen 2:19. The LORD God had formed every beast of the field and every bird of the heavens and brought them to the man to see what he would call them. And whatever the man called every living creature, that was its name.

Question 46. Did Adam rule over his dominion properly?

Adam failed to rule his dominion as God commanded and fell into sin.

Gen 3:17-19. And to Adam [God] said, "Because you have listened to the voice of your wife and have eaten of the tree of which I commanded you, 'You shall not eat of it,' cursed is the ground because of you; in

---

4. In Gen 2:15, "work" and "keep" translate the Hebrew verbs 'abad and shamar, respectively. Elsewhere in the Hebrew Bible, these Hebrew words refer to the priestly duties to "serve" and "guard" the sanctuary of God. For 'abad, see Num 3:7–8; 4:30; 7:5; 8:15; 16:9; 18:6, 21, 23. For shamar, see Num 1:53; 3:28, 32, 38; 18:5; Ezek 44:8, 15.

pain you shall eat of it all the days of your life; thorns and thistles it shall bring forth for you; and you shall eat the plants of the field. By the sweat of your face you shall eat bread, till you return to the ground, for out of it you were taken; for you are dust, and to dust you shall return."

Rom 5:12. Therefore, just as sin came into the world through one man.

Question 47. When did the heavenly sons of God sin?

The heavenly sons of God appear to have sinned in stages: some at or before the temptation of Adam,[a] some in the days before the flood,[b] and some after the flood.[c]

[a] **Ezek 28:13–15**. You were in Eden, the garden of God ... You were an anointed guardian cherub. I placed you; you were on the holy mountain of God ... You were blameless in your ways from the day you were created, till unrighteousness was found in you.

[b] **Gen 6:1–2, 4**. When man began to multiply on the face of the land and daughters were born to them, the sons of God saw that the daughters of man were attractive. And they took as their wives any they chose. The Nephilim were on the earth in those days and also afterward, when the sons of God came in to the daughters of man and they bore children to them.

2 Pet 2:4–5. For if God did not spare angels when they sinned, but cast them into hell and committed them to chains of gloomy darkness to be kept until the judgment; ⁵ if he did not spare the ancient world, but preserved Noah.

Jude 6. And the angels who did not stay within their own position of authority, but left their proper dwelling, he has kept in eternal chains under gloomy darkness until the judgment of the great day.

ᶜ **Rev 12:4–5, 7.** the dragon stood before the woman who was about to give birth, so that when she bore her child he might devour it. She gave birth to a male child, one who is to rule all the nations with a rod of iron ... Now war arose in heaven, Michael and his angels fighting against the dragon. And the dragon and his angels fought back.

Question 48. Who tempted Eve in the garden of Eden?

Eve was tempted by a member of God's divine council who was present in Eden since the council meets at the divine abode.⁵ This divine being is described with various Hebrew terms: *nahash*, a word used for "serpent" (noun),ᵃ "dispense divine knowledge through divination"

---

5. See question 37.

(verbal),[b; 6] and "shining" (adjective);[c; 7] *karub*, a cherub throne guardian whose appearance was like glistening gems;[d] *helel ben-shahar* ("morning star, son of the dawn").[e]

a   **Gen 3:1.** Now the serpent (*nahash*) was more crafty than any other beast of the field that the LORD God had made.

   Gen 3:13. The woman said, "The serpent (*nahash*) deceived me, and I ate."

b   **Gen 44:5.** Is it not from this that my lord drinks, and by this that he practices divination (*nahesh ynahesh*)?

   Lev 19:26 (JPS). You shall not practice divination (*tnachashu*) or soothsaying.

c   **Ezek 1:7.** [The] legs [of the cherubim] ... sparkled like burnished bronze (*nhoshet*).

   Dan 10:5–6. I lifted up my eyes and looked, and behold, a man clothed in linen ... His body was like beryl, his face like the appearance of lightning, his eyes like flaming torches, his arms and legs like the gleam of burnished bronze (*nhoshet*).

---

6. See *HALOT*, 690.

7. The examples in c are from *nehoshet*, a word that shares its root with *nahash*. The form *ha-nahash* found in Gen 3:1 can be translated "the shining one" (if a verbal root *nahash* is presumed—as opposed to a noun—the form would be a substantive participle in Hebrew).

d **Ezek 28:13-14.** You were in Eden, the garden of God; every precious stone was your covering sardius, topaz, and diamond, beryl, onyx, and jasper, sapphire, emerald, and carbuncle; and crafted in gold were your settings and your engravings. On the day that you were created they were prepared. You were an anointed guardian cherub (*krub*). I placed you; you were on the holy mountain of God; in the midst of the stones of fire you walked.

e **Isa 14:12.** "How you are fallen from heaven, O Day Star, son of Dawn!"

Question 49. Why did this divine being rebel against God's will and tempt our first parents?

He arrogantly wanted to rule in place of God,[a] rejecting the authority and wishes of his Creator, and the authority the Creator had given to Adam and Eve in the earthly location of the council.[8] Since humans had been created a little lower than *'elohim*,[b] he deemed them inferior and unworthy of inclusion in Yahweh's rule.

a **Isa 14:12-13.** How you are fallen from heaven, O Day Star, son of Dawn! ... You said in your heart, "I will ascend to heaven; above the stars of God I will set my

---

8. See question 37.

throne on high; I will sit on the mount of assembly in the far reaches of the north."

Ezek 28:13-15. You were in Eden, the garden of God ... You were an anointed guardian cherub. I placed you; you were on the holy mountain of God ... You were blameless in your ways from the day you were created, till unrighteousness was found in you.

b **Pss 8:4-5.** What is man that you are mindful of him, and the son of man that you care for him? Yet you have made him a little lower than the heavenly beings (*'elohim*) and crowned him with glory and honor.[9]

Question 50. How were Adam and Eve and the divine tempter able to rebel against God in Eden?

Lesser created divine beings were also created as God's imagers,[10] therefore sharing his attributes. Like humans, those attributes included a will.[11] Both humans and divine beings freely choose to follow their desires and transgress the Creator's will.

---

9. Cp. Heb 2:7: "You made him for a little while lower than the angels."
10. God said in Gen 1:26, "let us create humankind in our image." The pronouns "us" and "our" are plural, indicating God was speaking to a group—his heavenly host, his divine council. God's audience was not the Trinity for reasons of Hebrew grammar, logical coherence, and theological orthodoxy. See *The Unseen Realm*, Chapters 5, 8–9.
11. See questions 43–44.

Gen 3:6. So when the woman saw that the tree was good for food, and that it was a delight to the eyes, and that the tree was to be desired to make one wise, she took of its fruit and ate, and she also gave some to her husband who was with her, and he ate.

Isa 14:13–14. You said in your heart, "I will ascend to heaven; above the stars of God I will set my throne on high; I will sit on the mount of assembly in the far reaches of the north; I will ascend above the heights of the clouds; I will make myself like the Most High."

1 John 3:8. Whoever makes a practice of sinning is of the devil, for the devil has been sinning from the beginning.

Question 51. Was the divine rebel and tempter in Eden Satan?

The name "Satan" derives from the Hebrew word *satan*, which means "adversary." The *nahash* ("serpent") of the garden of Eden is never called *satan* in the Old Testament.[12] In the New Testament, however, the word became a title used for the great enemy of God in Eden, whose rebellion

---

12. The *satan* of Job is not the Devil. Job 1–2 never links him to the garden story. The serpent (*nahash*) was cast down to earth away from the presence of God and his council, to rule the underworld realm of the dead. The term *satan* in Job is also not a proper personal name, by rule of Hebrew grammar. The *satan* of Job is a divine council figure who behaves in an adversarial way, challenging God's knowledge and authority and, in the end, is shown to be wrong. See *The Unseen Realm*, Chapter 8.

made him deserving of the title "Adversary." In accord with the New Testament, we call this rebel Satan and the Devil.

> **Eph 6:11.** Put on the whole armor of God, that you may be able to stand against the schemes of the devil.

> **1 Pet 5:8.** Be sober-minded; be watchful. Your adversary the devil prowls around like a roaring lion, seeking someone to devour.

> **Rev 12:9.** The great dragon was thrown down, that ancient serpent, who is called the devil and Satan, the deceiver of the whole world.

Question 52. What happened to the Serpent (nahash) after his role in the garden?

The *nahash* was cursed, cast down to rule the realm of the dead in the underworld.[a; 13] He and his seed were cursed to die separated from God's presence.[b] The curse of this death was upon all humankind,[c] but would eventually be undone by the seed of the woman.[d]

> [a] **Gen 3:14.** On your belly you shall go, and dust you shall eat all the days of your life.

> **Isa 14:12, 15.** How you are fallen from heaven, O Day Star, son of Dawn! How you are cut down to the ground,

---

13. See *The Unseen Realm*, Chapters 11 and 12.

you who laid the nations low! ... You are brought down to Sheol, to the far reaches of the pit.

Ezek 28:13–16. You were in Eden, the garden of God. ... You were anointed guardian cherub. ... You were blameless in your ways from the day you were created, till unrighteousness was found in you ... so I cast you as a profane thing from the mountain of God, and I destroyed you, O guardian cherub, from the midst of the stones of fire.

[b] **Matt 25:41.** Then he will say to those on his left, "Depart from me, you cursed, into the eternal fire prepared for the devil and his angels."

Rev 19:20. And the beast was captured, and with it the false prophet who in its presence had done the signs by which he deceived those who had received the mark of the beast and those who worshiped its image. These two were thrown alive into the lake of fire that burns with sulfur.

Rev 20:14. Then Death and Hades were thrown into the lake of fire. This is the second death, the lake of fire.

ᶜ **Rom 5:12.** Therefore, just as sin came into the world through one man, and death through sin, and so death spread to all men with the result that all have sinned.[14]

ᵈ **Gen 3:15.** I will put enmity between you and the woman, and between your offspring and her offspring; he shall bruise your head, and you shall bruise his heel.

Luke 10:18. [Jesus] said to them, "I saw Satan fall like lightning from heaven."[15]

Rom 16:20. The God of peace will soon crush Satan under your feet.

Question 53. Who are the seed of the Serpent (nahash)?

The seed of the serpent are the spiritual offspring of the devil, all who willfully oppose God, his will, and his people.[16]

---

14. The translation follows ESV, save for the ending "with the result that all have sinned." For this translation, see C. E. B. Cranfield, "On Some of the Problems in the Interpretation of Rom 5.12–21," *Scottish Journal of Theology* 22 (1969): 324–341.

15. See *The Unseen Realm*, Chapter 32.

16. Though there is no scriptural evidence that the Nephilim and the later giant clans are the direct spawn of the serpent (*nahash*). In their willful opposition to God's will, they are the seed of the Serpent as well as the product of the divine transgression of the rebellious sons of God (Gen 6:1–4). See Section VI.

John 8:44. You [Pharisees] are of your father the devil, and your will is to do your father's desires.

Acts 13:10. You son of the devil, you enemy of all righteousness, full of all deceit and villainy, will you not stop making crooked the straight paths of the Lord?

1 Thess 5:5. You [church of Thessalonica] are all children of light, children of the day. We are not of the night or of the darkness.

1 John 3:12. We should not be like Cain, who was of the evil one.

PART 6

REBELLION BEFORE THE FLOOD

Question 54. Who were the sons of God of Genesis 6:1-4?

They were divine beings (*'elohim*)[1] who transgressed the boundary between the realms of heaven and earth, thereby sinning against God's will.

Jude 6. And the angels who did not stay within their own position of authority, but left their proper dwelling, he has kept in eternal chains under gloomy darkness until the judgment of the great day.

---

1. See question 13 and Section II.

2 Pet 2:4. For if God did not spare angels when they sinned, but cast them into hell and committed them to chains of gloomy darkness to be kept until the judgment.

Question 55. How did the sons of God transgress God's will?

Before the flood the heavenly sons of God cohabited with the daughters of men, forsaking their own realm or normal domain.[2]

Gen 6:1–2. When man began to multiply on the face of the land and daughters were born to them, the sons of God saw that the daughters of man were attractive. And they took as their wives any they chose.

Question 56. What was God's response to this transgression?

God imprisoned the offending sons of God below the earth, somewhere in the gloomy underworld realm of the dead, to await final judgment at the last day.

1 Pet 3:19–20. [Christ] went and proclaimed to the spirits in prison, because they formerly did not obey, when God's patience waited in the days of Noah.

---

2. See *The Unseen Realm*, Chapters 12 and 13.

2 Pet 2:4. God did not spare angels when they sinned, but cast them into hell and committed them to chains of gloomy darkness to be kept until the judgment.

Jude 6. The angels who did not stay within their own position of authority, but left their proper dwelling, he has kept in eternal chains under gloomy darkness until the judgment of the great day.

Question 57. Does Jesus teach that angels (that is, heavenly beings) cannot have sexual relations?

No. In Matt 22:30,[3] Jesus is referring to angels *in heaven*, not those who come to earth. Jesus words indicate that angels in heaven do not engage in such activities, but do not deny they can come to earth and assume flesh, with its natural abilities. Elsewhere the Bible teaches that angels can assume physical flesh with its normal functions, including eating and physical conflict—activities that are also unnecessary *in heaven*.[4]

Gen 18:2–5, 8. [Abraham] lifted up his eyes and looked, and behold, three men were standing in front of him.

---

3. Matthew 22:30 reads, "For in the resurrection they neither marry nor are given in marriage, but are like angels in heaven."

4. Some presume that when Jesus says, "a spirit does not have flesh and bones" (Luke 24:39) he aims to deny angels have had physical relations with women. But the error there is the same. The Bible clearly teaches that some spirits (divine beings) come to earth and assume flesh with its normal abilities and functions.

When he saw them, he ran from the tent door to meet them and bowed himself to the earth and said, "O Lord, if I have found favor in your sight, do not pass by your servant. Let a little water be brought, and wash your feet, and rest yourselves under the tree, while I bring a morsel of bread, that you may refresh yourselves, and after that you may pass on." ... Then he took curds and milk and the calf that he had prepared, and set it before them. And he stood by them under the tree while they ate.

Gen 19:1, 5, 9–11. The two angels came to Sodom in the evening, and Lot was sitting in the gate of Sodom. When Lot saw them, he rose to meet them and bowed himself with his face to the earth ... They called to Lot, "Where are the men who came to you tonight? Bring them out to us, that we may know them." ... Then they pressed hard against the man Lot, and drew near to break the door down. But the men reached out their hands and brought Lot into the house with them and shut the door. And they struck with blindness the men who were at the entrance of the house.

Gen 32:24–28, 30. And Jacob was left alone. And a man wrestled with him until the breaking of the day. ... And [the man] said to [Jacob], "What is your name?" And he said, "Jacob." Then he said, "Your name shall no longer be called Jacob, but Israel, for you have striven with God and with men, and have prevailed." ... So Jacob called the name of the place Peniel, saying, "For I have seen God face to face."

Hos 12:2-4. The LORD has an indictment against Judah and will punish Jacob according to his ways; he will repay him according to his deeds. In the womb he took his brother by the heel, and in his manhood he strove with God. He strove with the angel and prevailed.

Jude 6-7. The angels who did not stay within their own position of authority, but left their proper dwelling, he has kept in eternal chains under gloomy darkness until the judgment of the great day—just as Sodom and Gomorrah and the surrounding cities ... likewise indulged in sexual immorality.

Question 58. Did the sons of God produce offspring with the daughters of mankind?

Yes. These offspring were called the Nephilim.[5]

Gen 6:4. The Nephilim were on the earth in those days, and also afterward, when the sons of God came in to the daughters of man and they bore children to them. These were the mighty men who were of old, the men of renown.

---

5. The most straightforward reading (and the one held by all ancient Jews and Christians until the late 4th century AD) was that of cohabitation. It is also possible the language of Gen 6:1-4 expresses the idea of a less explicit divine intervention. See *The Unseen Realm*, Chapters 12 and 13.

Jude 6-7. The angels who did not stay within their own position of authority, but left their proper dwelling, he has kept in eternal chains under gloomy darkness until the judgment of the great day—just as Sodom and Gomorrah and the surrounding cities ... *likewise* indulged in sexual immorality.

Question 59. Who were these Nephilim?

The Nephilim were giants,[a] from whom the later giant clans who opposed Moses, Joshua, and the Israelites during the conquest of Canaan, and which contained remnants which were later destroyed by David and his mighty men.[b; 6]

[a] **Num 13:32-33.** All the people that we saw in it are of great height. And there we saw the Nephilim (the sons of Anak, who come from the Nephilim), and we seemed to ourselves like grasshoppers, and so we seemed to them.

[b] **Deut 2:10-11.** The Emim formerly lived there, a people great and many, and tall as the Anakim. Like the Anakim they are also counted as Rephaim, but the Moabites call them Emim.

Deut 3:11. For only Og the king of Bashan was left of the remnant of the Rephaim. Behold, his bed was a bed

---

6. See *The Unseen Realm*, Chapters 23-25. The word *Nephilim* itself means "giant" (See *The Unseen Realm*, Chapter 13).

of iron. Is it not in Rabbah of the Ammonites? Nine cubits was its length, and four cubits its breadth, according to the common cubit.

Amos 2:9-10. Yet it was I who destroyed the Amorite before them, whose height was like the height of the cedars and who was as strong as the oaks; I destroyed his fruit above and his roots beneath. Also it was I who brought you up out of the land of Egypt and led you forty years in the wilderness, to possess the land of the Amorite.[7]

2 Sam 21:22. These four were descended from the giants in Gath, and they fell by the hand of David and by the hand of his servants.

Question 60. Do these later giant clans—other Nephilim—have names?

The clans descended from the Nephilim include the Rephaim,[a] Zamzummim,[b] Emim,[c] and Anakim.[d; 8]

---

7. See Deut 2:24.

8. Some would include the Avvim on the basis of Deut 2:23 and Josh 13:3. Neither verse specifically describes their size, though they are mentioned along with the Philistines, who either came from Caphtor or settled there (Jer 47:4). Deuteronomy 2:23 seems to suggest the Avvim were displaced by the Caphtorim ("As for the Avvim, who lived in villages as far as Gaza, the Caphtorim, who came from Caphtor, destroyed them and settled in their place"). For an explanation of how other tribes fit into the giant puzzle, see Douglas Van Dorn, *Giants: Sons of the Gods* (Erie, CO: Waters of Creation Pub., 2013).

[a] **Deut 2:20-21.** Rephaim formerly lived there ... a people great and many and tall.

2 Sam 12:22. These four [Goliath, Ishbi-benob, Saph, and a giant with six toes and fingers] were descended from the giants (*rephaim*) in Gath, and they fell by the hand of David and by the hand of his servants.

[b] **Deut 2:20-21.** Rephaim formerly lived there—but the Ammonites call them Zamzummim—a people great and many, and tall as the Anakim.

[c] **Deut 2:10-11.** The Emim formerly lived there, a people great and many, and tall as the Anakim. Like the Anakim they are also counted as Rephaim, but the Moabites call them Emim.

[d] **Deut 1:28.** The people are greater and taller than we. The cities are great and fortified up to heaven. And besides, we have seen the sons of the Anakim there.

Josh 11:22. None of the Anakim [were] left in the land of the people of Israel. Only in Gaza, in Gath, and in Ashdod did some remain.

Josh 14:15. Now the name of Hebron formerly was Kiriath-arba. (Arba was the greatest man among the Anakim).

Josh 15:14. Caleb drove out from there the three sons of Anak, Sheshai and Ahiman and Talmai, the descendants of Anak.

Question 61. What else is known of the Rephaim?

Rephaim, ancient Nephilim who inhabited the land of Canaan after the flood,[a] are called the great dead heroes of old.[b] They became shades[c] or shadows of the underworld.[d; 9]

a **Num 13:33.** And there we saw the Nephilim (the sons of Anak, who come from the Nephilim).

Deut 2:11. Like the Anakim they are also counted as Rephaim, but the Moabites call them Emim.

Deut 3:13. The rest of Gilead, and all Bashan, the kingdom of Og, that is, all the region of Argob, I gave to the half-tribe of Manasseh. (All that portion of Bashan is called the land of Rephaim.)

b **Isa 14:9.** Sheol beneath is stirred up to meet you when you come; it rouses the shades (*rephaim*) to greet you, all who were leaders of the earth; it raises from their thrones all who were kings of the nations.

c **Isa 26:14.** They are dead, they will not live; they are shades (*rephaim*), they will not arise; to that end you

---

9. This description creates a biblical link between the spirits of dead Nephilim (Rephaim) and demons who inhabit the same underworld realm of the dead. The origin of demons is nowhere else alluded to in the Bible, and the belief that they were the spirits of dead Nephilim was pervasive in intertestamental Judaism. See question 74.

have visited them with destruction and wiped out all remembrance of them.

d **Isa 14:9**. Sheol beneath is stirred up to meet you when you come; it rouses the shades (*rephaim*) to greet you, all who were leaders of the earth; it raises from their thrones all who were kings of the nations.

Question 62. Why did the LORD destroy the earth in the flood?

The LORD destroyed the earth in the flood because the sons of God left their proper domain,[a] which led to the willful proliferation of human wickedness on the earth.[b; 10]

a **Gen 6:4.** The Nephilim were on the earth in those days, and also afterward, when the sons of God came in to the daughters of man and they bore children to them. These were the mighty men who were of old, the men of renown.

Jude 6. The angels who did not stay within their own position of authority, but left their proper dwelling.

---

10. Another consequence of the transgression of Gen 6:1–4 is that the human line of Eve that would produce the seed who would undo the failure of Eden was imperiled with extinction or corruption by the fallen sons of God. Ultimately, the genealogical line of Jesus extended through Noah (Luke 3:36).

[b] **Gen 6:5.** The LORD saw that the wickedness of man was great in the earth.

Gen 6:12. God saw the earth, and behold, it was corrupt, for all flesh had corrupted their way on the earth.

Question 63. Did some of the Nephilim survive the flood?

Yes, the Nephilim lineage is found after the flood.[11]

Gen 6:4. The Nephilim were on the earth in those days, and also afterward.

Num 13:33. And there we saw the Nephilim (the sons of Anak, who come from the Nephilim).

Question 64. Why are these giant stories in the Bible?

The giant stories tell us about the war between the two seeds,[a] a war that Israel never finally wins[b] but ultimately leads to their spiritual apostasy and exile. In this way, these stories prepare us for the coming Great Seed of Eve, the Lord and Savior Jesus Christ who alone wins the war against the seed of the serpent, whether divine or human.[c]

---

11. See *The Unseen Realm*, Chapter 23, for the possible explanations for this survival.

[a] **Gen 3:15**. I will put enmity between you and the woman, and between your offspring and her offspring; he shall bruise your head, and you shall bruise his heel.

Gen 14:1–16. Abraham, the seed, fights giants.

1 Sam 17. David, the seed, fights Goliath.

[b] **Judg 1:19, 21, 27, 28, 29, 30, 31, 32, 33**. They could not drive out the inhabitants [of Canaan].

[c] **Gal 4:4**. When the fullness of time had come, God sent forth his Son, born of woman.

PART 7

REBELLION AFTER THE FLOOD

Question 65. What happened to Noah and his family after the flood?

The sons of Noah had children, which eventually populated seventy nations listed in the Bible.

Gen 10:1, 32. These are the generations of the sons of Noah, Shem, Ham, and Japheth. Sons were born to them after the flood. ... These are the clans of the sons of Noah, according to their genealogies, in their nations, and from these the nations spread abroad on the earth after the flood.

Question 66. What did God command Noah and his sons do after the flood?

God repeated the command that he had given Adam and Eve to fill the earth[a] and reaffirmed that humankind still had dominion over the life on earth.[b]

[a] **Gen 9:1, 7.** God blessed Noah and his sons and said to them, "Be fruitful and multiply and fill the earth. ... Be fruitful and multiply, increase greatly on the earth and multiply in it."

[b] **Gen 9:2–3.** The fear of you and the dread of you shall be upon every beast of the earth and upon every bird of the heavens, upon everything that creeps on the ground and all the fish of the sea. Into your hand they are delivered. Every moving thing that lives shall be food for you. And as I gave you the green plants, I give you everything.

Question 67. Did the descendants of Noah's sons obey God's command?

Initially they did, migrating from the east. However, against God's command, they eventually decided to settle in Shinar (Babylon) to build a tower as the place where God could be summoned[1] and to make themselves famous.[2]

> **Gen 11:1-2, 4.** Now the whole earth had one language and the same words. And as people migrated from the east, they found a plain in the land of Shinar and settled there. ... Then they said, "Come, let us build ourselves a city and a tower with its top in the heavens, and let us make a name for ourselves, lest we be dispersed over the face of the whole earth."

Question 68. What was God's response to this disobedience and presumption?

God confused their language[a] and divided the people into the nations that ultimately became the basis for the list of

---

1. Scholars are agreed that the tower of Babylon was a ziggurat, an artificial cosmic mountain that was part of temple complexes throughout Mesopotamia. By building this structure, the dispersion halted, and humankind sought to control their relationship with God. Temples were places where the divine presence resided. God had not commanded them to do this, nor was he a God who could be summoned by human will.

2. The phrase "to make for ourselves a name" is an echo of the Name (God) in that, instead of aligning themselves with the will of the Name, they seek to magnify their own name. This is the backdrop for the later commands to not bear ("take up," translating the Hebrew word *nasa'*) the name of the Lord in vain (Exod 20:7), to depart from iniquity if one names the name of Christ (2 Tim 2:19), and the fact that God's great eschatological enemy brands his followers with his own name (Rev 13:17, the name of the Beast).

nations in Gen 10. God then allotted the nations to the authority of lesser *'elohim* (sons of God).[b; 3]

[a] **Gen 11:7–8.** [God said,] "Come, let us go down and there confuse their language, so that they may not understand one another's speech." So the LORD dispersed them from there over the face of all the earth, and they left off building the city.

[b] **Deut 4:19.** And beware lest you raise your eyes to heaven, and when you see the sun and the moon and the stars, all the host of heaven, you be drawn away and bow down to them and serve them, things that the LORD your God has allotted to all the peoples under the whole heaven.

Deut 32:8. When the Most High gave to the nations their inheritance, when he divided mankind, he fixed the borders of the peoples according to the number of the sons of God.[4]

---

3. See *The Unseen Realm*, Chapter 14. This division produced a worldview of cosmic geography, where Israel was holy ground and all other places were under dominion of hostile *'elohim* spirits. See question 33.
4. For the reading "sons of God," see page 17, footnote 3.

Question 69. Having given the nations over to be ruled by the sons of God, did God intend that the nations worship these other gods and so deprive them of knowledge of the true God?

No, the true God allotted the gods to the nations in judgment, but he did not entirely abandon them. He has revealed his desire that they would learn of him through the blessings of creation,[a] search for him,[b] and ultimately find him through the promised Seed of Eve.[c] But the gods corrupted the nations rather than ruling them justly to prepare them to seek the true God.[d]

[a] **Acts 14:16–17.** In past generations he allowed all the nations to walk in their own ways. Yet he did not leave himself without witness, for he did good by giving you rains from heaven and fruitful seasons, satisfying your hearts with food and gladness.

[b] **Acts 17:26–27** LEB. [God] made from one *man* every nation of humanity to live on all the face of the earth, determining *their* fixed times and the fixed boundaries of their habitation, to search for God, if perhaps indeed they might feel around for him and find *him*. And indeed he is not far away from each one of us.

[c] **Luke 24:46–47.** Thus it is written, that the Christ should suffer and on the third day rise from the dead, and that repentance and forgiveness of sins should be

proclaimed in his name to all nations, beginning from Jerusalem.

Gal 3:7–9, 13–16, 26–29. Know then that it is those of faith who are the sons of Abraham. And the Scripture, foreseeing that God would justify the Gentiles by faith, preached the gospel beforehand to Abraham, saying, "In you shall all the nations be blessed." So then, those who are of faith are blessed along with Abraham, the man of faith. ... Christ redeemed us from the curse of the law by becoming a curse for us—for it is written, "Cursed is everyone who is hanged on a tree"—so that in Christ Jesus the blessing of Abraham might come to the Gentiles, so that we might receive the promised Spirit through faith. To give a human example, brothers: even with a man-made covenant, no one annuls it or adds to it once it has been ratified. Now the promises were made to Abraham and to his offspring.[5] It does not say, "And to offsprings," referring to many, but referring to one, "And to your offspring," who is Christ. ... in Christ Jesus you are all sons of God, through faith. For as many of you as were baptized into Christ have put on Christ. There is neither Jew nor Greek, there is neither slave nor free, there is no male and female, for you are all one in Christ Jesus. And if you are Christ's, then you are Abraham's offspring, heirs according to promise.

---

5. The Greek word is *sperma* ("seed").

^d **Pss 82:1-4**. God has taken his place in the divine council; in the midst of the gods he holds judgment: "How long will you judge unjustly and show partiality to the wicked? Give justice to the weak and the fatherless; maintain the right of the afflicted and the destitute. Rescue the weak and the needy; deliver them from the hand of the wicked."

Question 70. What else did these corrupt sons of God do that offended the true God?

Instead of stewarding the nations to prepare them to seek the true God, the corrupt sons of God seduced God's own people, Israel, to worship them and so commit idolatry.

Deut 4:19. And beware lest you raise your eyes to heaven, and when you see the sun and the moon and the stars, all the host of heaven, you be drawn away and bow down to them and serve them.

Deut 17:2-3. If there is found among you ... a man or woman who does what is evil in the sight of the LORD your God, in transgressing his covenant, and has gone and served other gods and worshiped them, or the sun or the moon or any of the host of heaven, which I have forbidden.

Deut 29:24-26. All the nations will say, "Why has the LORD done thus to this land? What caused the heat of this great anger?" Then people will say, "It is because they abandoned the covenant of the LORD, the God of their fathers, which he made with them when he brought them out of the land of Egypt, and went and served other gods and worshiped them, gods whom they had not known and whom he had not allotted to them."

Deut 32:17 NASB. They sacrificed to demons who were not God, To gods whom they have not known.[6]

Question 71. How are these corrupt sons of God and their allotted dominions referred to in the New Testament?

The heavenly sons of God assigned over the nations God disinherited at Babel are described with many terms, including rulers and princes,[a; 7] cosmic powers and authorities,[b] lords,[c] and thrones and dominions.[d]

a **Eph 2:1-2**. And you were dead in the trespasses and sins in which you once walked, following the course of this world, following the prince of the power of the air.

1 Cor 2:7-8. We impart a secret and hidden wisdom of God, which God decreed before the ages for our glory. None of the rulers of this age understood this, for if they had, they would not have crucified the Lord of glory.

---

6. See question 73.

7. For OT background, see Dan 10:13: "The prince of the kingdom of Persia withstood [the angel Gabriel] twenty-one days, but Michael, one of the chief princes, came to help me, for I was left there with the kings of Persia."

b **Eph 3:10**. ... so that through the church the manifold wisdom of God might now be made known to the rulers and authorities in the heavenly places.

Eph 6:12. For we do not wrestle against flesh and blood, but against the rulers, against the authorities, against the cosmic powers over this present darkness, against the spiritual forces of evil in the heavenly places.

Rom 8:38–39. For I am sure that neither death nor life, nor angels nor rulers, nor things present nor things to come, nor powers ... will be able to separate us from the love of God.

c **1 Cor 8:5**. Indeed there are many "gods" and many "lords."

d **Col 1:16**. For by him all things were created, in heaven and on earth, visible and invisible, whether thrones or dominions or rulers or authorities—all things were created through him and for him.

Question 72. Are these corrupt sons of God demons or fallen angels?

The sons of God who sinned before the flood were imprisoned until the end, and so they are not the demons of the New Testament. The corrupt sons of God put over the nations are called *shedim,* a term of geographical guardianship.[8] Therefore, demons are neither fallen angels nor the offending sons of God, yet they belong to the same spirit world because they are disembodied spirits.[9]

> **1 Pet 3:19-20.** [Christ] went and proclaimed to the spirits in prison, because they formerly did not obey, when God's patience waited in the days of Noah.

> **2 Pet 2:4.** God did not spare angels when they sinned, but cast them into hell and committed them to chains of gloomy darkness to be kept until the judgment.

> **Jude 6.** The angels who did not stay within their own position of authority, but left their proper dwelling, he has kept in eternal chains under gloomy darkness until the judgment of the great day.

Question 73. What does the word "demon" mean?

The word "demon" comes from two related Greek words: *daimon* and *daimonion*. Both words are general terms for a divine being—a being that inhabits the spirit

---

8. See questions 74–75.

9. In the Hebrew Bible, the inclusive term for any resident of the disembodied spirit world is *'elohim*, while terms like "angel" and "sons of God" refer to a spirit's function or hierarchical status (see questions 26–27). In the New Testament, the Greek word *aggelos* ("angel") is generically used for disembodied beings, whether good (Matt 4:11; 24:31; 2 Thess 1:7) or evil (Matt 25:41; Rev 12:9). That term therefore functions similarly to the Old Testament's *'elohim*. Two other terms (*daimon, daimonion* ["demon"]) are also used generically for evil spirits, though outside the Bible those two terms can refer to any disembodied being.

world—whether good or evil.[10] In the New Testament, these terms are used of evil ("unclean") spirits.

> **Matt 8:16**. That evening they brought to [Jesus] many who were oppressed by demons, and he cast out the spirits with a word and healed all who were sick.

> **Matt 12:28, 43-45**. But if it is by the Spirit of God that I cast out demons, then the kingdom of God has come upon you. ... When the unclean spirit has gone out of a person, it passes through waterless places seeking rest, but finds none. Then it says, "I will return to my house from which I came." And when it comes, it finds the house empty, swept, and put in order. Then it goes and brings with it seven other spirits more evil than itself.

> **Luke 4:33**. And in the synagogue there was a man who had the spirit of an unclean demon.

Question 74. What is the origin of demons?

Demons are the disembodied spirits of dead Nephilim.[a; 11] They are therefore by nature disembodied, which is why they seek to inhabit other things.[b]

---

10. See *The Unseen Realm*, Chapter 37.

11. See question 61. Intertestamental Jewish literature (for example, *1 Enoch*) that the New Testament writers Peter (2 Pet 2:4–5) and Jude (Jude 6–7) draw upon for their understanding of the events of Gen 6:1–4 has much to say about this point of origin (see *1 Enoch* 15). The idea is suggested in the verses referenced above.

^a **Num 13:33.** And there we saw the Nephilim (the sons of Anak, who come from the Nephilim).

Deut 2:11. Like the Anakim they are also counted as Rephaim, but the Moabites call them Emim.

Deut 3:13. The rest of Gilead, and all Bashan, the kingdom of Og, that is, all the region of Argob, I gave to the half-tribe of Manasseh. (All that portion of Bashan is called the land of Rephaim.)

Isa 14:9. Sheol beneath is stirred up to meet you when you come; it rouses the shades (*rephaim*) to greet you, all who were leaders of the earth; it raises from their thrones all who were kings of the nations.

Isa 26:14. They are dead, they will not live; they are shades (*rephaim*), they will not arise; to that end you have visited them with destruction and wiped out all remembrance of them.

^b **Matt 8:28.** And when he came to the other side, to the country of the Gadarenes, two demon-possessed men met him, coming out of the tombs.

Matt 12:28, 43–45. But if it is by the Spirit of God that I cast out demons, then the kingdom of God has come upon you. ... When the unclean spirit has gone out of a person, it passes through waterless places seeking rest, but finds none. Then it says, "I will return to my house from which I came." And when it comes, it finds the house empty, swept, and put in order. Then it goes and brings with it seven other spirits more evil than itself.

Mark 5:10-13. And he begged him earnestly not to send them out of the country. Now a great herd of pigs was feeding there on the hillside, and they begged him, saying, "Send us to the pigs; let us enter them." So he gave them permission. And the unclean spirits came out and entered the pigs; and the herd, numbering about two thousand, rushed down the steep bank into the sea and drowned in the sea.

Question 75. Does the Hebrew word translated "demon" in the Old Testament[12] describe the same evil spirits the New Testament describes as "demons"?

No. The sinister divine beings of Deut 32:17 (*shedim*) are those set over the nations (Deut 32:8), who seduced the Israelites into idolatry. They are never described as Nephilim or the disembodied spirits of Nephilim.

---

12. This Hebrew word (*shed*; plural: *shedim*) occurs only two times in the entire Old Testament: Deut 32:17 and Pss 106:37. These two verses refer to the corrupt sons of God put over the nations in judgment at Babel (see question 66) who seduced the Israelites into worshipping them (see question 68). The term comes from Akkadian *shadu*, which describes a guardian spirit (including over geography, which fits the context of Deut 32:8 and the resulting judgment at Babel quite well). Consequently, the geographical turf guardians of Deut 32:17 are not the disembodied spirits that come from the Nephilim killed in the flood, which are the demons (see question 72). English translations have at times created confusion on these points.

PART 8

THE PROMISE ANTICIPATED

Question 76. What is Israel?

The nation of Israel was the physical seed of Abraham, raised up out of nothing by the LORD to be his own inheritance, after he had disinherited the rebellious nations at Babel. Israel is therefore the people of God, distinct and separate from the peoples (nations) of the other gods.

Gen 12:1-2. Now the LORD said to Abram, ... "I will make of you a great nation."

Gen 32:28. Then he said, "Your name shall no longer be called Jacob, but Israel, for you have striven with God and with men, and have prevailed."

Deut 32:8-9. When the Most High gave to the nations their inheritance, when he divided mankind, he fixed the borders of the peoples according to the number of the sons of God. But the LORD's portion is his people, Jacob his allotted heritage.

Exod 19:6. You shall be to me a kingdom of priests and a holy nation. These are the words that you shall speak to the people of Israel.

Question 77. Was Israel therefore the son of God?

Yes. The Scriptures call the people of Israel God's son.

Exod 4:22 NASB. Israel is My son, My first-born.

Hos 11:1. When Israel was a child, I loved him, and out of Egypt I called my son.

Question 78. How then is the Messiah the son of God?

The messiah is the son of God because he is the son of David, the rightful king, who is called by God "my son."[a] The king is the representative of the people of Israel, who are collectively God's son.[b] Israel is called God's servant,[c] but God also sends a servant who suffers for the sins of God's people in order to redeem Israel.[d]

[a] **Pss 2:7-8**. I will tell of the decree: The LORD said to me, "You are my Son; today I have begotten you. Ask of me, and I will make the nations your heritage, and the ends of the earth your possession."

[b] **Exod 4:22** NASB. Israel is My son, My first-born.

Hos 11:1. When Israel was a child, I loved him, and out of Egypt I called my son.

c **Isa 44:1-2.** But now hear, O Jacob my servant, Israel whom I have chosen! ... Fear not, O Jacob my servant, Jeshurun whom I have chosen.

Isa 44:21. Remember these things, O Jacob, and Israel, for you are my servant; I formed you; you are my servant; O Israel, you will not be forgotten by me.

d **Isa 53:11.** Out of the anguish of his soul he shall see and be satisfied; by his knowledge shall the righteous one, my servant, make many to be accounted righteous, and he shall bear their iniquities.

Question 79. Who is the seed of the woman that God promised in Gen 3:15?

The seed of the woman can be defined on three levels. In the broadest terms, it refers to humanity in general.[a] More specifically, the seed of the woman is Abraham's offspring in the flesh (that is, Israel). Most specifically, the seed of the woman is the messiah, the son of David and a descendent of Abraham,[b] through whom all of God's people from both Israel and the disinherited nations are redeemed and made victorious over death,[c] thereby escaping the consequences of failure of Adam in Eden.[d]

a **Gen 4:1-2.** Now Adam knew Eve his wife, and she conceived and bore Cain, saying, "I have gotten a man with the help of the LORD." And Again, she bore his brother Abel.

Acts 17:26, 28. And he made from one man every nation of mankind ... for "In Him we live and move and have our being"; as even some of your own poets have said, "For we are indeed his offspring."

[b] **Luke 3:23, 31-32, 34-38.** Jesus, when he began his ministry, was about thirty years of age, being the son (as was supposed) of Joseph, the son of Heli ... the son of Melea, the son of Menna, the son of Mattatha, the son of Nathan, the son of David, the son of Jesse ... the son of Jacob, the son of Isaac, the son of Abraham ... the son of Cainan, the son of Arphaxad, the son of Shem, the son of Noah, the son of Lamech, the son of Methuselah, the son of Enoch, the son of Jared, the son of Mahalaleel, the son of Cainan, the son of Enos, the son of Seth, the son of Adam, the son of God.

Rom 1:1-4. Paul, a servant of Christ Jesus, called to be an apostle, set apart for the gospel of God, which he promised beforehand through his prophets in the holy Scriptures, concerning his Son, who was descended from David according to the flesh and was declared to be the Son of God in power according to the Spirit of holiness by his resurrection from the dead, Jesus Christ our Lord.

[c] **Luke 24:47**. "Thus it is written, that the Christ should suffer and on the third day rise from the dead, and

that repentance and forgiveness of sins should be proclaimed in his name to all nations, beginning from Jerusalem.

Gal 4:4. When the fullness of time had come, God sent forth his Son, born of woman.

[d] **Heb 2:14-15**. Since therefore the children share in flesh and blood, [Jesus] himself likewise partook of the same things, that through death he might destroy the one who has the power of death, that is, the devil.

1 Cor 15:42-45. So is it with the resurrection of the dead. What is sown is perishable; what is raised is imperishable. It is sown in dishonor; it is raised in glory. It is sown in weakness; it is raised in power. It is sown a natural body; it is raised a spiritual body. If there is a natural body, there is also a spiritual body. Thus it is written, "The first man Adam became a living being"; the last Adam became a life-giving spirit.

Question 80. How does the promised seed of the woman differ from other embodied sons of God in the Old Testament?

The promised messianic seed is not merely embodied in flesh but was the LORD incarnate,[a] the second person of the holy Trinity born of a virgin[b] and not through carnal physical relations between a lesser god (*'elohim*) and a woman.[c] He is therefore fully man and fully God rather than a demi-god (half god, half man).[d]

ᵃ **Phil 2:5-8**. Have this mind among yourselves, which is yours in Christ Jesus, who, though he was in the form of God, did not count equality with God a thing to be grasped, but emptied himself, by taking the form of a servant, being born in the likeness of men. And being found in human form, he humbled himself by becoming obedient to the point of death, even death on a cross.

ᵇ **Matt 1:23**. Behold, the virgin shall conceive and bear a son, and they shall call his name Immanuel"(which means, God with us).

Luke 1:34-35. Mary said to the angel, "How will this be, since I am a virgin?" The angel answered her, "The Holy Spirit will come upon you, and the power of the Most High will overshadow you."

ᶜ **Gen 6:1-2, 4**. When man began to multiply on the face of the land and daughters were born to them, the sons of God saw that the daughters of man were attractive. And they took as their wives any they chose. ... The Nephilim were on the earth in those days and also afterward, when the sons of God came in to the daughters of man and they bore children to them.

ᵈ **John 1:1-3**. In the beginning was the Word, and the Word was with God, and the Word was God.

John 1:14 NASB. The Word became flesh, and dwelt among us, and we beheld His glory, glory as of the only begotten from the Father, full of grace and truth.

John 1:17–18. For the law was given through Moses; grace and truth came through Jesus Christ. No one has ever seen God; the only God, who is at the Father's side, he has made him known.

John 20:28. Thomas answered [Jesus], "My Lord and my God!"

1 John 4:2–3. By this you know the Spirit of God: every spirit that confesses that Jesus Christ has come in the flesh is from God, and every spirit that does not confess Jesus is not from God. This is the spirit of the antichrist.

Question 81. Could not Satan and the other hostile powers of darkness have refused to kill the messiah, thereby thwarting God's plan?

They could have if had they known the plan. But God in his wisdom made the plan a mystery, scattering its elements in many places in the Scriptures, never revealing its coherence in complete form. For this reason, both men and gods discerned only the most obvious component: God would send his messiah to be an earthly deliverer-king to restore the throne of David. However, neither men nor gods suspected[1] that this plan would be accom-

---

1. See *The Unseen Realm*, Chapters 28 and 33.

plished by the messiah's atoning death rather than a military deliverance.

1 Cor 2:7-8. But we impart a secret and hidden wisdom of God, which God decreed before the ages for our glory. None of the rulers of this age understood this, for if they had, they would not have crucified the Lord of glory.

Mark 9:30-32. They went on from there and passed through Galilee. And he did not want anyone to know, for he was teaching his disciples, saying to them, "The Son of Man is going to be delivered into the hands of men, and they will kill him. And when he is killed, after three days he will rise." But they did not understand the saying, and were afraid to ask him.

Luke 24:44-45. [After the resurrection,] he said to them, "These are my words that I spoke to you while I was still with you, that everything written about me in the Law of Moses and the Prophets and the Psalms must be fulfilled." Then he opened their minds to understand the Scriptures.

PART 9

THE PROMISE FULFILLED

Question 82. How was Jesus the promised seed?

Jesus was God's servant,[a] sent to redeem Israel from an exile caused by her disloyalty and sinful idolatry, and the heir to the throne of David.[b]

[a] **Isa 49:3-5**. And [the LORD] said to me, "You are my servant, Israel, in whom I will be glorified." But I said, "I have labored in vain; I have spent my strength for nothing and vanity; yet surely my right is with the LORD, and my recompense with my God." And now the LORD says, he who formed me from the womb to be his servant, to bring Jacob back to him; and that Israel might be gathered to him.

Isa 53:10-11. Yet it was the will of the LORD to crush him; he has put him to grief; when his soul makes an offering for guilt, he shall see his offspring; he shall prolong his days; the will of the LORD shall prosper in his hand. Out of the anguish of his soul he shall see and be satisfied; by his knowledge shall the righteous one, my servant, make many to be accounted righteous, and he shall bear their iniquities.

Luke 24:46-47. Thus it is written, that the Christ should suffer and on the third day rise from the dead, and that repentance and forgiveness of sins should be proclaimed in his name to all nations, beginning from Jerusalem.

Gal 4:4. When the fullness of time had come, God sent forth his Son, born of woman.

b **Matt 1:1.** The book of the genealogy of Jesus Christ, the son of David, the son of Abraham.

Matt 16:15-17. [Jesus] said to them, "But who do you say that I am?" Simon Peter replied, "You are the Christ, the Son of the living God." And Jesus answered him, "Blessed are you, Simon Bar-Jonah! For flesh and blood has not revealed this to you, but my Father who is in heaven.

Mark 12:35-37. And as Jesus taught in the temple, he said, "How can the scribes say that the Christ is the son of David? David himself, in the Holy Spirit, declared, 'The Lord said to my Lord, "Sit at my right hand, until I put your enemies under your feet." ' David himself calls him Lord. So how is he his son?"

Luke 2:10-11. And the angel said to them, "Fear not, for behold, I bring you good news of great joy that will be for all the people. For unto you is born this day in the city of David a Savior, who is Christ the Lord.

Question 83. How is Jesus superior to Adam, the original seed and son of God in Eden?

Whereas the first Adam failed to fulfill his Edenic roles (prophet, priest, and king), Jesus was the sinless[a] prophet, priest, and king,[1] and so he inherited all authority in heaven and on earth as one who is above all powers.[b]

[a] **2 Cor 5:21.** For our sake [God] made [Jesus] to be sin who knew no sin, so that in him we might become the righteousness of God.

1 Pet 2:22. [Jesus] committed no sin, neither was deceit found in his mouth.

[b] **Eph 1:18-23.** ... that you may know ... what is the immeasurable greatness of [God's] power toward us who believe, according to the working of his great might that he worked in Christ when he raised him from the dead and seated him at his right hand in the heavenly places, far above all rule and authority and power and dominion, and above every name that is named, not only in this age but also in the one to come. And he put all things under his feet and gave him as head over all

---

1. See questions 45–46.

things to the church, which is his body, the fullness of him who fills all in all.

1 Pet 3:22. [Christ] has gone into heaven and is at the right hand of God, with angels, authorities, and powers having been subjected to him.

Question 84. How did Jesus defeat Satan and all other infernal powers?

Jesus withstood and bound the hostile powers of darkness in his life;[a] he disarmed and triumphed over them at the cross in his death[b] and proclaimed victory over them in his resurrection.[c] He rules over them in his ascension[d] and through his Church,[e] and he will finally and totally destroy them in his glorious Second Coming.[f]

[a] **Matt 4:10–11.** Jesus said to him, "Be gone, Satan! For it is written, 'You shall worship the Lord your God and him only shall you serve.'" Then the devil left him, and behold, angels came and were ministering to him.

Matt 12:27–29. If I cast out demons by Beelzebul, by whom do your sons cast them out? Therefore they will be your judges. But if it is by the Spirit of God that I cast out demons, then the kingdom of God has come upon you. Or how can someone enter a strong man's house and plunder his goods, unless he first binds the strong man? Then indeed he may plunder his house.

Heb 2:14–15. Since therefore the children share in flesh and blood, he himself likewise partook of the same things, that through death he might destroy the one who has the power of death, that is, the devil, and deliver all those who through fear of death were subject to lifelong slavery.

[b] **Luke 4:18.** He has sent me to proclaim liberty to the captives.

Col 2:14-15. He disarmed the rulers and authorities and put them to open shame, by triumphing over them in him.

1 Cor 2:8. None of the rulers of this age understood this, for if they had, they would not have crucified the Lord of glory.

[c] **1 Pet 3:18-19.** Christ also suffered once for sins, the righteous for the unrighteous, that he might bring us to God, being put to death in the flesh but made alive in the spirit, in which he went and proclaimed to the spirits in prison.

[d] **Eph 1:20-21.** [The Father of glory] worked in Christ when he raised him from the dead and seated him at his right hand in the heavenly places, far above all rule and authority and power and dominion, and above every name that is named, not only in this age but also in the one to come.

Eph 4:8. When he ascended on high he led a host of captives, and he gave gifts to men.

1 Pet 3:21–22. Jesus Christ, who has gone into heaven and is at the right hand of God, with angels, authorities, and powers having been subjected to him.

e **Eph 1:22.** He put all things under his feet and gave him as head over all things to the church.

Eph 3:10. Through the church the manifold wisdom of God might now be made known to the rulers and authorities in the heavenly places.

f **Isa 24:21.** On that day the LORD will punish the host of heaven, in heaven, and the kings of the earth, on the earth.

Matt 8:28–29 NIV. Two demon-possessed men coming from the tombs met him. They were so violent that no one could pass that way. "What do you want with us, Son of God?" they shouted. "Have you come here to torture us before the appointed time?"

Rev 20:10. The devil who had deceived them was thrown into the lake of fire.

Rev 20:14. Death and Hades were thrown into the lake of fire. This is the second death, the lake of fire.

Question 85. How did Jesus have authority over Satan, the gods of the nations, and demons?

Since Jesus is one with the Father, God incarnate, Lord of the divine council[a; 2] and sovereign creator of all things visible and invisible,[b] he has authority over all other created *'elohim*.

[a] **Pss 82:1, 6–7.** God has taken his place in the divine council; in the midst of the gods he holds judgment. ... You are gods, sons of the Most High, all of you; nevertheless, like men you shall die, and fall like any prince.

John 10:30–38.[3] [Jesus said,] "I and the Father are one." ... The Jews picked up stones again to stone him. Jesus answered them, "I have shown you many good works from the Father; for which of them are you going to stone me?" The Jews answered him, "It is not for a good work that we are going to stone you but for blasphemy, because you, being a man, make yourself God." Jesus answered them, "Is it not written in your Law, 'I said, you are gods'? If he called them gods to whom the word of God came—and Scripture cannot be broken—do you say of him whom the Father consecrated and sent into the world, 'You are blaspheming,' because I said, 'I am the Son of God'? If I am not doing the works of my Father, then do not believe me; but if I do them, even

---

2. See questions 24, 39–41.

3. See the note on John 10:34–35 in *The Unseen Realm*, Chapter 21.

though you do not believe me, believe the works, that you may know and understand that the Father is in me and I am in the Father."

[b] **Pss 33:6**. By the word of the LORD the heavens were made, and by the breath of his mouth all their host.

Col 1:16. By him all things were created, in heaven and on earth, visible and invisible, whether thrones or dominions or rulers or authorities—all things were created through him and for him.

Question 86. How did Jesus undo Adam's failure, which had brought death to all humankind?

As God incarnate[a] Jesus became the second Adam, fulfilled the demands of the Law[b] and the covenants as the promised seed,[4] died in the place of all those who had not and could not,[c] and then rose from the grave. By his life, death, and resurrection, he conquered death[d] and exempted believers from the second death, Satan's claim on them as lord of the dead.[e]

[a] **John 1:1**. In the beginning was the Word, and the Word was with God, and the Word was God.

John 1:17-18. For the law was given through Moses; grace and truth came through Jesus Christ. No one has

---

4. See questions 82–83.

ever seen God; the only God, who is at the Father's side, he has made him known.

Rom 9:5. The Christ who is God over all, blessed forever. Amen.

Heb 1:2. In these last days he has spoken to us by his Son, whom he appointed the heir of all things, through whom also he created the world.

[b] **Matt 5:17.** Do not think that I have come to abolish the Law or the Prophets; I have not come to abolish them but to fulfill them.

Rom 10:4. For Christ is the end of the law for righteousness to everyone who believes.

Gal 3:13. Christ redeemed us from the curse of the law by becoming a curse for us.

[c] **Matt 20:28**. The Son of Man came not to be served but to serve, and to give his life as a ransom for many.

1 Tim 2:5–6. For there is one God, and there is one mediator between God and men, the man Christ Jesus, who gave himself as a ransom for all, which is the testimony given at the proper time.

Rom 5:8–9, 15. But God shows his love for us in that while we were still sinners, Christ died for us. Since, therefore, we have now been justified by his blood, much more shall we be saved by him from the wrath of God. ... But the free gift is not like the trespass. For if many died through one man's trespass, much more have the grace of God and the free gift by the grace of that one man Jesus Christ abounded for many.

1 Cor 15:45. Thus it is written, "The first man Adam became a living being"; the last Adam became a life-giving spirit.

d **Heb 2:14**. Since therefore the children share in flesh and blood, [Jesus] himself likewise partook of the same things, that through death he might destroy the one who has the power of death, that is, the devil.

1 Cor 15:42-45. So is it with the resurrection of the dead. What is sown is perishable; what is raised is imperishable. It is sown in dishonor; it is raised in glory. It is sown in weakness; it is raised in power. It is sown a natural body; it is raised a spiritual body. If there is a natural body, there is also a spiritual body. Thus it is written, "The first man Adam became a living being"; the last Adam became a life-giving spirit.

e **Rev 20:6**. Blessed and holy is the one who shares in the first resurrection! Over such the second death has no power.

Question 87. What is the kingdom of Christ?

The kingdom of Christ is the kingdom of God. It was inaugurated during Jesus' life when he presented himself as the king on earth,[a] was offered up according to God's plan, and then rose from the dead. His kingdom continues in the heavenly dominion and authority of the risen

King, Jesus, who is ruling over our present evil age from the right hand of God.[b]

[a] **Matt 4:17.** From that time Jesus began to preach, saying, "Repent, for the kingdom of heaven is at hand."

Matt 10:5-7. These twelve Jesus sent out, instructing them, "Go nowhere among the Gentiles and enter no town of the Samaritans, but go rather to the lost sheep of the house of Israel. And proclaim as you go, saying, 'The kingdom of heaven is at hand.'"

Matt 12:28. But if it is by the Spirit of God that I cast out demons, then the kingdom of God *has come* upon you.[5]

Luke 17:20-21. Being asked by the Pharisees when the kingdom of God would come, he answered them, "The kingdom of God is not coming in ways that can be observed, nor will they say, 'Look, here it is!' or 'There!' for behold, the kingdom of God is in the midst of you."

[b] **Matt 28:18-19.** All authority in heaven and on earth has been given to [Jesus]. Go therefore and make disciples of all nations.

Eph 1:18-23. ... that you may know ... what is the immeasurable greatness of [God's] power toward us who believe, according to the working of his great might that he worked in Christ when he raised him from the

---

5. Emphasis added.

dead and seated him at his right hand in the heavenly places, far above all rule and authority and power and dominion, and above every name that is named, not only in this age but also in the one to come. And he put all things under his feet and gave him as head over all things to the church, which is his body, the fullness of him who fills all in all.

1 Pet 3:22. [Christ] has gone into heaven and is at the right hand of God, with angels, authorities, and powers having been subjected to him.

Question 88. Who are the members of this kingdom?

While every created person and thing is under the dominion of the risen Christ, believers enjoy membership[a] in his kingdom, having been adopted[b] into his family through faith in his gracious work on the cross.

a **Rom 14:17.** For the kingdom of God is not a matter of eating and drinking but of righteousness and peace and joy in the Holy Spirit.

Col 1:13-14. [God] has delivered us from the domain of darkness and transferred us to the kingdom of his beloved Son, in whom we have redemption, the forgiveness of sins.

2 Pet 1:10-11. Therefore, brothers, be all the more diligent to confirm your calling and election, for if you practice these qualities you will never fall. For in this way there will be richly provided for you an entrance into the eternal kingdom of our Lord and Savior Jesus Christ.

Heb 12:28-29. Therefore let us be grateful for receiving a kingdom that cannot be shaken, and thus let us offer to God acceptable worship, with reverence and awe, for our God is a consuming fire.

b **John 1:12.** But to all who did receive him, who believed in his name, he gave the right to become children of God.

Rom 8:14-16. For all who are led by the Spirit of God are sons of God. For you did not receive the spirit of slavery to fall back into fear, but you have received the Spirit of adoption as sons, by whom we cry, "Abba! Father!" The Spirit himself bears witness with our spirit that we are children of God.

Gal 4:4-7. But when the fullness of time had come, God sent forth his Son, born of woman, born under the law, to redeem those who were under the law, so that we might receive adoption as sons. And because you are sons, God has sent the Spirit of his Son into our hearts, crying, "Abba! Father!" So you are no longer a slave, but a son, and if a son, then an heir through God.

Question 89. What is the Church?

The Church is the believing people of God, the new Israel,[6] the members of God's kingdom, and the scriptural fulfillment of God's purposes for Old Testament Israel that the nations ("Gentiles") would be reclaimed through the promised seed, the messiah son of Abraham and David.[a] In this way, people from all nations are being included in the totality of the people of God according to God's plan.[b]

[a] **Gen 12:1-3.** Now the LORD said to Abram, ... "I will make of you a great nation. ... and in you all families of the earth shall be blessed."

Gal 3:7-9, 13-16, 26-29. Know then that it is those of faith who are the sons of Abraham. And the Scripture, foreseeing that God would justify the Gentiles by faith, preached the gospel beforehand to Abraham, saying, "In you shall all the nations be blessed." So then, those who are of faith are blessed along with Abraham, the man of faith. ... Christ redeemed us from the curse of the law by becoming a curse for us—for it is written, "Cursed is everyone who is hanged on a tree"— so that in Christ Jesus the blessing of Abraham might come to the Gentiles, so that we might receive the promised Spirit through faith. To give a human example,

---

6. This is not to say that there *may not be* further eschatological destiny for ethnic/national Israel. Scripture affirms that the Church is the new Israel, but the New Testament use of the term "Israel" does not exclusively speak of the Church.

brothers: even with a man-made covenant, no one annuls it or adds to it once it has been ratified. Now the promises were made to Abraham and to his offspring.[7] It does not say, "And to offsprings," referring to many, but referring to one, "And to your offspring," who is Christ. ... [F]or in Christ Jesus you are all sons of God, through faith. For as many of you as were baptized into Christ have put on Christ. There is neither Jew nor Greek, there is neither slave nor free, there is no male and female, for you are all one in Christ Jesus. And if you are Christ's, then you are Abraham's offspring, heirs according to promise.

Gal 6:16. Peace and mercy be upon them, and upon the Israel of God.

Rom 2:28. A Jew is one inwardly, and circumcision is a matter of the heart, by the Spirit, not by the letter. His praise[8] is not from man but from God.

Rom 4:13-16. For the promise to Abraham and his offspring that he would be heir of the world did not come through the law but through the righteousness of faith.

---

7. The Greek word is *sperma* ("seed").

8. "Praise" here is a wordplay on "Jew." The term "Jew" is short for Judah, the son of Jacob and the southern portion of the divided kingdom that contained Jerusalem and the Temple. Judah means "praise," deriving from the Hebrew verb *yadah*, "to praise." This connection is clear at the naming of Judah in Genesis: "And she conceived again and bore a son, and said, 'This time I will praise [*'odeh*, from *yadah*] the LORD.' Therefore she called his name Judah" (Gen 29:35).

For if it is the adherents of the law who are to be the heirs, faith is null and the promise is void. For the law brings wrath, but where there is no law there is no transgression. That is why it depends on faith, in order that the promise may rest on grace and be guaranteed to all his offspring—not only to the adherent of the law but also to the one who shares the faith of Abraham, who is the father of us all.

Rom 9:6-7. Not all who are descended from Israel belong to Israel, ... not all are children of Abraham because they are his offspring, but "Through Isaac shall your offspring be named."

1 Pet 2:9. You are a chosen race, a royal priesthood, a holy nation, a people for his own possession.

b **Gen 17:4.** Behold, my covenant is with you [Abraham], and you shall be the father of a multitude of nations.

Pss 2:7-8. I will tell of the decree: The LORD said to me, "You are my Son; today I have begotten you. Ask of me, and I will make the nations your heritage, and the ends of the earth your possession."

Pss 82:8. Arise, O God, judge the earth; for you shall inherit all the nations!

Isa 66:19-21. "I will set a sign among them. And from them I will send survivors to the nations, to Tarshish, Pul, and Lud, who draw the bow, to Tubal and Javan, to the coastlands far away, that have not heard my fame or seen my glory. And they shall declare my glory among the nations. And they shall bring all your brothers from all the nations as an offering to the LORD, on horses and in chariots and in litters and on mules and on dromedaries, to my holy mountain Jerusalem," says the LORD, "just as the Israelites bring their grain offering in a clean vessel to the house of the LORD. And some of them also I will take for priests and for Levites," says the LORD.

Heb 1:2. In these last days he has spoken to us by his Son, whom he appointed the heir of all things.

Question 90. What is the kingdom of Christ yet to come?

The kingdom of Christ is already present although not completely in its final form; it will be revealed in its fullness in the age to come, the last days, in the new and glorious global Eden, the kingdom of God on earth.

Matt 24:14. And this gospel of the kingdom will be proclaimed throughout the whole world as a testimony to all nations, and then the end will come.

Matt 26:29. I tell you I will not drink again of this fruit of the vine until that day when I drink it new with you in my Father's kingdom.

Acts 1:6–8. So when they had come together, they asked him, "Lord, will you at this time restore the kingdom to Israel?" He said to them, "It is not for you to know times or seasons that the Father has fixed by his own authority. But you will receive power when the Holy Spirit has come upon you, and you will be my witnesses in Jerusalem and in all Judea and Samaria, and to the end of the earth."

1 Cor 15:23-24. But each in his own order: Christ the firstfruits, then at his coming those who belong to Christ. Then comes the end, when he delivers the kingdom to God the Father after destroying every rule and every authority and power. For he must reign until he has put all his enemies under his feet. The last enemy to be destroyed is death.

2 Tim 4:1. I charge you in the presence of God and of Christ Jesus, who is to judge the living and the dead, and by his appearing and his kingdom.

2 Pet 1:11. For in this way there will be richly provided for you an entrance into the eternal kingdom of our Lord and Savior Jesus Christ.

Rev 22:1-2. Then the angel showed me the river of the water of life, bright as crystal, flowing from the throne of God and of the Lamb through the middle of the street of the city; also, on either side of the river, the tree of life with its twelve kinds of fruit, yielding its fruit each month. The leaves of the tree were for the healing of the nations.

Question 91. What is a believer's destiny in the kingdom to come?

Those who believe in Jesus, in the good news of his work on the cross, will be co-rulers with him, under his authority, finally displacing the rebellious gods placed over the nations.

> **Rev 2:25–28.** Only hold fast what you have until I come. The one who conquers and who keeps my works until the end, to him I will give authority over the nations, and he will rule them with a rod of iron, as when earthen pots are broken in pieces, even as I myself have received authority from my Father. And I will give him the morning star.[9]

> **Rev 3:20–21.** Behold, I stand at the door and knock! If anyone hears my voice and opens the door, indeed I will come in to him and dine with him, and he with me. The one who conquers, I will grant to him to sit down with me on my throne, as I also have conquered and have sat down with my Father on his throne.

> **1 Cor 6:2–3.** Do you not know that the saints will judge the world? And if the world is to be judged by you, are you incompetent to try trivial cases? Do you not know that we are to judge angels? How much more, then, matters pertaining to this life!

---

9. See *The Unseen Realm*, Chapters 35 and 42.

PART 10

THE GOOD NEWS

Question 92. What takes people out from under the dark deception and tyrannical kingdom of Satan and the fallen gods, and brings them into the kingdom of Christ?

The good news, which is the gospel of Jesus Christ, brings believer's into the kingdom of Christ.

> **Isa 40:9.** Get you up to a high mountain, O Zion, herald of good news; lift up your voice with strength, O Jerusalem, herald of good news; lift it up, fear not; say to the cities of Judah, "Behold your God!"

> **Acts 8:12.** He preached good news about the kingdom of God and the name of Jesus Christ.

> **Acts 26:16-18, 20.** I [Jesus] have appeared to you for this purpose, to appoint you as a servant and witness to the things in which you have seen me and to those

in which I will appear to you, delivering you from your people and from the Gentiles—to whom I am sending you to open their eyes, so that they may turn from darkness to light and from the power of Satan to God, that they may receive forgiveness of sins and a place among those who are sanctified by faith in me, ... declared first to those in Damascus, then in Jerusalem and throughout all the region of Judea, and also to the Gentiles.

Rom 1:16. For I am not ashamed of the gospel, for it is the power of God for salvation to everyone who believes.

Question 93. What is this gospel?

The gospel is the announcement of the truth that Jesus Christ, the eternal Son of God[1] and the promised Seed of the woman,[2] has paid the ransom for sin,[a] defeated death,[b] nullified Satan's claim on humanity as lord of the dead by bearing our sins,[c] and appeased the wrath of God.[d] On account of Christ's faithfulness, God offers the imputation of Christ's righteousness to all,[e] bringing them peace with God and everlasting life as children of God[f] if they will turn to Christ in repentance and faith.

---

1. See Qs. 7 and 24.
2. See Qs. 78 and 80.

[a] **1 Pet 2:24.** He himself bore our sins in his body on the tree, that we might die to sin and live to righteousness.

Mark 10:45. For even the Son of Man came not to be served but to serve, and to give his life as a ransom for many.

1 Tim 2:6. Who gave himself as a ransom for all.

[b] **Heb 2:14-15.** Since therefore the children share in flesh and blood, [Jesus] himself likewise partook of the same things, that through death he might destroy the one who has the power of death, that is, the devil.

1 Cor 15:42-45. So is it with the resurrection of the dead. What is sown is perishable; what is raised is imperishable. It is sown in dishonor; it is raised in glory. It is sown in weakness; it is raised in power. It is sown a natural body; it is raised a spiritual body. If there is a natural body, there is also a spiritual body. Thus it is written, "The first man Adam became a living being"; the last Adam became a life-giving spirit.

[c] **1 Pet 2:24.** He himself bore our sins in his body on the tree, that we might die to sin and live to righteousness. By his wounds you have been healed.

Heb 9:28. Christ, having been offered once to bear the sins of many, will appear a second time, not to deal with sin but to save those who are eagerly waiting for him.

^d **John 3:36.** Whoever believes in the Son has eternal life; whoever does not obey the Son shall not see life, but the wrath of God remains on him.

1 Thess 5:9–10. For God has not destined us for wrath, but to obtain salvation through our Lord Jesus Christ, who died for us so that whether we are awake or asleep we might live with him.

^e **Rom 3:21–22.** But now the righteousness of God has been manifested apart from the law, although the Law and the Prophets bear witness to it—the righteousness of God through faith in Jesus Christ for all who believe.

Phil 3:8–9. Indeed, I count everything as loss because of the surpassing worth of knowing Christ Jesus my Lord. For his sake I have suffered the loss of all things and count them as rubbish, in order that I may gain Christ and be found in him, not having a righteousness of my own that comes from the law, but that which comes through faith in Christ, the righteousness from God that depends on faith.

2 Pet 1:1–2. Simeon Peter, a servant and apostle of Jesus Christ, To those who have obtained a faith of equal standing with ours by the righteousness of our God and Savior Jesus Christ.

^f **John 3:16–18.** For God so loved the world, that he gave his only Son, that whoever believes in him should not perish but have eternal life. For God did not send his

Son into the world to condemn the world, but in order that the world might be saved through him. Whoever believes in him is not condemned, but whoever does not believe is condemned already, because he has not believed in the name of the only Son of God.

Question 94. What happens when the news of the victory of the gospel of Christ's kingdom is delivered?

Satan and the demons are cast out and trampled underfoot by the members of Christ's kingdom[3] who are empowered by the Spirit, boldly proclaiming the gospel of Jesus Christ,[a] properly observing baptism and the Lord's Supper,[b] and maintaining the purity in their own lives and their believing communities (that is, local churches).[c]

[a] **1 Cor 2:2, 4-8.** For I decided to know nothing among you except Jesus Christ and him crucified ... my speech and my message were not in plausible words of wisdom, but in demonstration of the Spirit and of power, so that your faith might not rest in the wisdom of men but in the power of God. Yet among the mature we do impart wisdom, although it is not a wisdom of this age or of the rulers of this age, who are doomed to pass away. But we impart a secret and hidden wisdom of God, which God decreed before the ages for our

---

3. See question 88.

glory. None of the rulers of this age understood this, for if they had, they would not have crucified the Lord of glory.

Rom 1:16. For I am not ashamed of the gospel, for it is the power of God for salvation to everyone who believes, to the Jew first and also to the Greek.

Rom 16:25-26. Now to him who is able to strengthen you according to my gospel and the preaching of Jesus Christ, according to the revelation of the mystery that was kept secret for long ages but has now been disclosed and through the prophetic writings has been made known to all nations, according to the command of the eternal God, to bring about the obedience of faith.

[b] **1 Cor 10:20-21.** I imply that what pagans sacrifice they offer to demons and not to God. I do not want you to be participants with demons. You cannot drink the cup of the Lord and the cup of demons. You cannot partake of the table of the Lord and the table of demons.

1 Cor 11:26. As often as you eat this bread and drink the cup, you proclaim the Lord's death until he comes.

Col 2:12-15. Having been buried with him in baptism, in which you were also raised with him through faith in the powerful working of God, who raised him from the dead. And you, who were dead in your trespasses and the uncircumcision of your flesh, God made alive together with him, having forgiven us all our trespasses, by canceling the record of debt that stood against us with its legal demands. This he set aside, nailing it to the cross. He disarmed the rulers and authorities and put them to open shame, by triumphing over them in him.

1 Pet 3:18-22. For Christ also suffered once for sins, the righteous for the unrighteous, that he might bring us to God, being put to death in the flesh but made alive in the spirit, in which he went and proclaimed to the spirits in prison, because they formerly did not obey, when God's patience waited in the days of Noah, while the ark was being prepared, in which a few, that is, eight persons, were brought safely through water. Baptism, which corresponds to this, now saves you, not as a removal of dirt from the body but as an appeal to God for a good conscience, through the resurrection of Jesus Christ, who has gone into heaven and is at the right hand of God, with angels, authorities, and powers having been subjected to him.

c **Matt 18:15-18.** If your brother sins against you, go and tell him his fault, between you and him alone. If he listens to you, you have gained your brother. But if he does not listen, take one or two others along with you, that every charge may be established by the evidence of two or three witnesses. If he refuses to listen to them, tell it to the church. And if he refuses to listen even to the church, let him be to you as a Gentile and a tax collector. Truly, I say to you, whatever you bind on earth shall be bound in heaven, and whatever you loose on earth shall be loosed in heaven.

1 Cor 5:5. Deliver this man to Satan for the destruction of the flesh, so that his spirit may be saved in the day of the Lord.

Eph 5:10–12. Try to discern what is pleasing to the Lord. Take no part in the unfruitful works of darkness, but instead expose them. For it is shameful even to speak of the things that they do in secret.

2 Tim 2:19. God's firm foundation stands, bearing this seal: "The Lord knows those who are his," and, "Let everyone who names the name of the Lord depart from iniquity."

Question 95. What then is your only comfort in life and in death?[4]

That I am not my own,[a] but belong—body and soul, in life and in death[b]—to my faithful Savior Jesus Christ;[c] who has fully paid for all my sins with his precious blood,[d] and has set me free from the tyranny of the devil.[e] He watches over me in such a way[f] that not a hair can fall from my head without the will of my Father in heaven;[g] in fact, all things must work together for my salvation,[h] because I

---

4. This is a reworking of the first question in the *Heidelberg Catechism*, my favorite of the great catechisms of the Reformation. I insert it here because it appropriately ends this primer.

belong to him, Christ assures me of eternal life by his Holy Spirit[i] and makes me wholeheartedly willing and ready from now on to live for him.[j]

[a] **1 Cor 6:19-20**. Or do you not know that your body is a temple of the Holy Spirit within you, whom you have from God? You are not your own, for you were bought with a price. So glorify God in your body.

[b] **Rom 14:7-9**. For none of us lives to himself, and none of us dies to himself. For if we live, we live to the Lord, and if we die, we die to the Lord. So then, whether we live or whether we die, we are the Lord's. For to this end Christ died and lived again, that he might be Lord both of the dead and of the living.

[c] **1 Cor 3:23**. You are Christ's, and Christ is God's.

Titus 2:14. [Christ] who gave himself for us to redeem us from all lawlessness and to purify for himself a people for his own possession who are zealous for good works.

[d] **1 Pet 1:18-19**. Knowing that you were ransomed from the futile ways inherited from your forefathers, not with perishable things such as silver or gold, but with the precious blood of Christ, like that of a lamb without blemish or spot.

1 John 2:2. He is the propitiation for our sins, and not for ours only but also for the sins of the whole world.

^e **John 8:34–35.** Jesus answered them, "Truly, truly, I say to you, everyone who practices sin is a slave to sin. The slave does not remain in the house forever; the son remains forever."

Heb 2:14–15. Since therefore the children share in flesh and blood, he himself likewise partook of the same things, that through death he might destroy the one who has the power of death, that is, the devil, and deliver all those who through fear of death were subject to lifelong slavery.

1 John 3:8–9. Whoever makes a practice of sinning is of the devil, for the devil has been sinning from the beginning. The reason the Son of God appeared was to destroy the works of the devil. No one born of God makes a practice of sinning, for God's seed abides in him, and he cannot keep on sinning because he has been born of God.

^f **John 6:39–40.** And this is the will of him who sent me, that I should lose nothing of all that he has given me, but raise it up on the last day. For this is the will of my Father, that everyone who looks on the Son and believes in him should have eternal life, and I will raise him up on the last day.

2 Thess 3:3. But the Lord is faithful. He will establish you and guard you against the evil one.

1 Pet 1:5. Who by God's power are being guarded through faith for a salvation ready to be revealed in the last time.

g **Matt 10:29-30**. Are not two sparrows sold for a penny? And not one of them will fall to the ground apart from your Father. But even the hairs of your head are all numbered.

Luke 21:16-18. You will be delivered up even by parents and brothers and relatives and friends, and some of you they will put to death. You will be hated by all for my name's sake. But not a hair of your head will perish.

h **Rom 8:28**. And we know that for those who love God all things work together for good, for those who are called according to his purpose.

i **Rom 8:15-16**. For you did not receive the spirit of slavery to fall back into fear, but you have received the Spirit of adoption as sons, by whom we cry, "Abba! Father!" The Spirit himself bears witness with our spirit that we are children of God.

2 Cor 1:21-22. And it is God who establishes us with you in Christ, and has anointed us, and who has also put his seal on us and given us his Spirit in our hearts as a guarantee.

Eph 1:13-14. In him you also, when you heard the word of truth, the gospel of your salvation, and believed in him, were sealed with the promised Holy Spirit, who is the guarantee of our inheritance until we acquire possession of it, to the praise of his glory.

ʲ **Rom 8:1–17.** There is therefore now no condemnation for those who are in Christ Jesus. For the law of the Spirit of life has set you free in Christ Jesus from the law of sin and death. For God has done what the law, weakened by the flesh, could not do. By sending his own Son in the likeness of sinful flesh and for sin, he condemned sin in the flesh, in order that the righteous requirement of the law might be fulfilled in us, who walk not according to the flesh but according to the Spirit. For those who live according to the flesh set their minds on the things of the flesh, but those who live according to the Spirit set their minds on the things of the Spirit. For to set the mind on the flesh is death, but to set the mind on the Spirit is life and peace. For the mind that is set on the flesh is hostile to God, for it does not submit to God's law; indeed, it cannot. Those who are in the flesh cannot please God.

You, however, are not in the flesh but in the Spirit, if in fact the Spirit of God dwells in you. Anyone who does not have the Spirit of Christ does not belong to him. But if Christ is in you, although the body is dead because of sin, the Spirit is life because of righteousness. If the Spirit of him who raised Jesus from the dead dwells in you, he who raised Christ Jesus from the dead will also give life to your mortal bodies through his Spirit who dwells in you.

So then, brothers, we are debtors, not to the flesh, to live according to the flesh. For if you live according to the flesh you will die, but if by the Spirit you put to death the deeds of the body, you will live. For all who are led by the Spirit of God are sons of God. For you did not receive the spirit of slavery to fall back into fear, but you have received the Spirit of adoption as sons, by whom we cry, "Abba! Father!" The Spirit himself bears witness with our spirit that we are children of God, and if children, then heirs—heirs of God and fellow heirs with Christ, provided we suffer with him in order that we may also be glorified with him.

Part 4 – Divine Council 41